COMPLE

LIBRARY OF MATHEMATICS

edited by
WALTER LEDERMANN
D.Sc., Ph.D., F.R.S.Ed., Professor of
Mathematics, University of Sussex

COMPLEX NUMBERS

BY

WALTER LEDERMANN

Routledge & Kegan Paul

LONDON AND HENLEY

First published 1960
in Great Britain by
Routledge & Kegan Paul Limited
39 Store Street
London WC1E 7DD and
Broadway House, Newtown Road
Henley-on-Thames, Oxon RG9 1EN
Printed in Great Britain by
Whitstable Litho Ltd., Whitstable, Kent

Second impression (with some corrections) 1962
Reprinted 1964, 1965, 1967, 1971 and 1976

ISBN 0 7100 4345 7

Preface

THE purpose of this book is to present a straightforward introduction to complex numbers and their properties. Complex numbers, like other kinds of numbers, are essentially objects with which to perform calculations according to certain rules, and when this principle is borne in mind, the nature of complex numbers is no more mysterious than that of the more familiar types of numbers. This formal approach has recently been recommended in a Report† prepared for the Mathematical Association. We believe that it has distinct advantages in teaching and that it is more in line with modern algebraical ideas than the alternative geometrical or kinematical definitions of $\sqrt{-1}$ that used to be proposed.

On the other hand, an elementary textbook is clearly not the place to enter into a full discussion of such questions as logical consistency, which would have to be included in a rigorous axiomatic treatment. However, the steps that had to be omitted (with due warning) can easily be filled in by the methods of abstract algebra, which do not conflict with the 'naïve' attitude adopted here.

I should like to thank my friend and colleague Dr. J. A. Green for a number of valuable suggestions, especially in connection with the chapter on convergence, which is a sequel to his volume *Sequences and Series* in this Library.

WALTER LEDERMANN

† *The Teaching of Algebra in Sixth Forms*, Chapter 3. (G. Bell & Sons, Ltd., London, 1957.)

Contents

CHAPTER ONE

Algebraic Theory of Complex Numbers

---

1. NUMBER SYSTEMS

Before defining complex numbers let us briefly review the more familiar types of numbers and let us examine why there are different kinds of numbers.

The most primitive type of number is the set of *natural numbers* 1, 2, 3, . . ., which the child learns for counting objects. Arithmetic, the science of numbers, is based on the fact that numbers can be added and multiplied, subject to certain rules, to which we shall presently return in more detail. It is the existence of these two laws of composition and their mutual relation that we shall regard as the typical feature of all numbers and that will serve us as a guide for introducing new systems of numbers for various purposes.

Let us recall how in the school curriculum we proceed from the natural numbers to more elaborate systems. The attempt to make subtraction always possible, that is to solve the equation $a+x=b$ for x when a and b are given, leads to the introduction of zero (one of the great achievements of the human mind!) and of the negative numbers. We now have the set of all *integers* (whole numbers) . . . -3, -2, -1, 0, 1, 2, 3, . . . Next, when we wish to carry out division, we have to solve equations of the form $ax=b$, where a and b are given integers and a is non-zero. In order to make the solution possible in all cases it is necessary to introduce the *rational numbers* (fractions). These numbers are denoted by symbols b/a, where a and b are integers and a is non-zero.

When this stage has been reached, the four rules of arithmetic, that is addition, subtraction, multiplication and division apply without restriction, always excepting division by zero. These basic operations are governed by the following general laws, which are of fundamental importance in mathematics.

    I. $a+b=b+a$ (**commutative law of addition**).

    II. $(a+b)+c=a+(b+c)$ (**associative law of addition**).

    III. $a+x=b$ has a unique solution, written $x=b-a$ (**law of subtraction**).

    IV. $ab=ba$ (**commutative law of multiplication**).

    V. $(ab)c=a(bc)$ (**associative law of multiplication**).

    VI. $ax=b$ $(a\neq 0)$ has a unique solution $x=b/a$ (**law of division**).

    VII. $(a+b)c=ac+bc$ (**distributive law**).

Most of these laws, perhaps in a different guise, are so familiar to the reader that he might be unaware of their existence. Thus the associative law of addition implies that a column of figures can be added by starting either from the top or from the bottom. Again, the distributive law is more popularly known as the principle of multiplying out brackets.

The rational numbers are adequate for dealing with the more elementary questions of arithmetic, but their deficiency becomes apparent when we consider such problems as extracting square roots. For example, it can be shown that $\sqrt 2$ cannot be expressed in the form m/n, where m and n are integers, *i.e.* there are no integers m, n $(\neq 0)$ such that $m^2=2n^2$. Again, when we pass from algebra to analysis, where limits of sequences play a fundamental part, we find that the limit of a sequence of rational numbers is not necessarily a rational number.† The situation may be described by using a single co-ordinate axis

† See J. A. Green, *Sequences and Series*, in this series, p. 7.

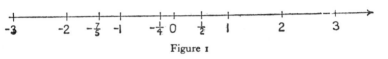

Figure 1

on which in the first place we mark all the integers in a certain scale. Then we imagine all the rational numbers inserted, e.g. $- 7/5$, $- 1/4$, $1/2$, ... But even when this has been done, there will be many points on the line against which no number has been entered. For instance when we lay down a segment of length $\sqrt{2}$ (the diagonal of a square of unit sides) by placing one end at 0, the other end-point falls on a point of the scale which has as yet no number attached to it. On the other hand, we intuitively accept the fact that every segment ought to have a length which is measured by some 'number'. In other words, we postulate that every point on the axis possesses a co-ordinate which is a definite number, positive if the point is on the right of 0 and negative if it is on the left of 0. This number need not be a rational number. The set of numbers which in this way fill the whole line, is called the set of *real* numbers; they comprise the familiar rational numbers, the remaining real numbers being called *irrational*, such as $\sqrt{2}$, e, π, log 2, etc. (Of course, the word irrational means that the number is not the *ratio* of two integers and has nothing to do with the idea that something irrational is beyond the realm of reason.) Alternatively, the real numbers may be described as the set of all decimal fractions. A terminating or a recurrent decimal fraction corresponds to a rational number, whilst the other fractions represent irrational numbers.

From the way in which real numbers are depicted on a line it is clear that there exists an *order relation* among them, that is any two real numbers a and b satisfy either $a = b$ or $a < b$ or $a > b$. This is indeed an important property when we wish to use numbers for measuring. But in the present algebraical context we are much more concerned with the fact that real numbers, like rational numbers, can be added

3

and multiplied and that they obey the laws I to VII listed on p. 2. We take the view that the existence of the two modes of composition with their laws makes numbers deserve their name. Numbers are essentially things to be computed, and any other properties, however useful for certain purposes, are not part of the definition of number. One of these secondary properties is the fact that real numbers can be classified into positive and negative numbers together with the usual deductions from it, such as 'the product of two negative numbers is positive'.

For a long time it was held that arithmetic had reached saturation with the introduction of the complete set of real numbers. Indeed, there was no obvious geometrical or technical problem that called for the creation of new numbers. Yet, one of the simplest algebraical questions remains in an unsatisfactory state when only real numbers are available. For we should then be forced to admit that some quadratic equations have solutions whilst others have none. On the other hand, it is easy to see that all quadratic equations would have solutions if only we could solve the special equation

$$x^2 + 1 = 0, \qquad (1.1)$$

for this would assign a meaning to $\sqrt{-1}$ and hence to $\sqrt{-a}$, where a is any positive number. Indeed, we could simply put $\sqrt{-a} = \sqrt{-1}\sqrt{a}$. Now it is obvious that (1.1) cannot have a real solution, since if x is real, x^2 is never negative and cannot therefore be equal to -1. So in order to make (1.1) soluble we have to introduce a new type of number, for which the rule 'the square of any number is positive' certainly does not hold. But this rule, or indeed anything else concerning positiveness and negativeness is not a consequence of the seven fundamental laws listed on p. 2, and it is therefore quite conceivable that these laws can be satisfied by symbols or numbers to which the terms positive and negative do not apply.

We now formally introduce a symbol i which we treat in

the same way as an indeterminate x in algebra, except that i has the additional property that

$$i^2 = -1. \tag{1.2}$$

More precisely, we (tentatively) postulate that when i is adjoined to the existing real numbers, addition and multiplication in the enlarged system will still obey the seven fundamental laws despite the bizarre stipulation (1.2). On this assumption, we deduce from (1.2) that

$$i^3 = -i, \ i^4 = 1, \ i^5 = i, \ i^6 = -1, \ldots \tag{1.3}$$

Thus a polynomial in i, that is an expression of the form $a_0 + a_1 i + a_2 i^2 + a_3 i^3 + a_4 i^4 + \ldots + a_n i^n$, where the co-efficients $a_0, a_1, \ldots, a_n$ are real, reduces to the simple form $a + ib$, where $a = a_0 - a_2 + a_4 - \ldots$ and $b = a_1 - a_3 + a_5 - \ldots$ are real numbers. A symbol of the form

$$\alpha = a + ib \text{ or } a + bi$$

where a and b are real, will be called a *complex number*. The algebraical and other properties of these numbers, as we shall feel justified in calling them, will be studied in the remainder of this book.

2. THE ALGEBRAIC THEORY

The first prerequisite for a set of objects to qualify as numbers is that they should be capable of being added and multiplied. The natural way to define addition is to put

$$(a + ib) + (c + id) = (a + c) + i(b + d), \tag{1.4}$$

collecting terms with i and terms without i. For example, $(3 + 2i) + (5 + 6i) = 8 + 8i$, $(-1 + 4i) + (2 + (-7)i) = 1 + (-3)i$. As regards multiplication, we obtain by formal multiplication

$$(a + ib)(c + id) = ac + adi + bci + bdi^2,$$

whence by (1.2),

$$(a + ib)(c + id) = (ac - bd) + i(ad + bc). \tag{1.5}$$

The definitions (1.4) and (1.5) constitute the basis for an

algebraical treatment of complex numbers. Although these definitions appear to be quite natural or even obvious, they can be accepted only if they are compatible with the seven fundamental laws. This is indeed the case, but the verification of this fact is somewhat tedious and we ask the reader to take it on trust.

A complex number $a+ib$ is completely given when the real numbers a and b are known. The numbers $a+ib$ and $c+id$ are equal if and only if simultaneously $a=c$ and $b=d$. Thus an equation involving complex numbers is equivalent to two equations between real numbers.

It is possible to think of a complex number as an *ordered pair* of real numbers (a, b), and the formulae $(1\cdot4)$ and $(1\cdot5)$ then correspond to rules for adding and multiplying such pairs. Thus

$$(a, b) + (c, d) = (a + c, b + d)$$
$$(a, b)(c, d) = (ac - bd, ad + bc).$$

However, we prefer to regard a complex number as a single mathematical entity and, whenever possible we use a single letter to denote a complex number, thus $\alpha = a + ib$.

The real numbers a and b are called the *real part* and the *imaginary part* of α respectively, and we write

$$a = \mathscr{R}\alpha, \quad b = \mathscr{I}\alpha.$$

Note that the imaginary part of α is in fact a real number. When $\mathscr{I}\alpha = 0$, the complex number α reduces to $a + i0$, and this symbol behaves in every way like the real number a. In this case the rules for addition and multiplication reduce to

$$(a + i0) + (c + i0) = a + c + i0$$
$$(a + i0)(c + i0) = ac + i0.$$

We shall therefore simply write a for $a + i0$ and we accordingly regard the real numbers as special cases of complex numbers, namely those complex numbers whose imaginary parts are zero. Note, in particular, that the multiplication of a complex number by a real number follows the simple rule.

$$a(c + id) = (c + id)a = ac + iad.$$

6

The complex zero and the complex unit are the same as the real 0 and 1. A complex number of the form ib, whose real part is zero is called a *purely imaginary* number. There is no need to comment on the contraction of notation whereby $a+(-b)i$ is written as $a-ib$. Subtraction is evidently given by the formula

$$(a+ib)-(c+id)=(a-c)+i(b-d).$$

We defer the discussion of division until we have introduced a few more useful concepts and formulae.

With every complex number $\alpha=a+ib$ we associate the *conjugate* complex number $\bar{\alpha}=a-ib$. Thus $\bar{\alpha}=\alpha$ means that α is real, that is $b=0$; $\bar{\alpha}=-\alpha$ holds if and only if α is purely imaginary. The passage from α to $\bar{\alpha}$ consists merely in replacing i by $-i$. It should be noted that every significant algebraical statement about i is also true about $-i$, because both symbols satisfy the defining relation $i^2=(-i)^2=-1$.

It is easy to verify the important rules

$$\overline{\alpha+\beta}=\bar{\alpha}+\bar{\beta} \tag{1.6}$$

$$\overline{\alpha\beta}=\bar{\alpha}\,\bar{\beta} \tag{1.7}$$

For example, (1.7) means explicitly that in the notation of (1.5) $(ac-bd)-i(ad+bc)=(a-ib)(c-id)$. In particular, we have that $\overline{\alpha^2}=(\bar{\alpha})^2$, etc. An interesting result is obtained when we multiply α by $\bar{\alpha}$, thus

$$\alpha\bar{\alpha}=(a+ib)(a-ib)=a^2-(ib)^2=a^2+b^2,$$

which is real and positive, except when $\alpha=0$, in which case it is obviously zero. The non-negative† real number

$$|\alpha|=\surd(a^2+b^2)=\surd\{(\mathscr{R}\alpha)^2+(\mathscr{I}\alpha)^2\} \tag{1.8}$$

is called the *modulus (absolute value)* of α, and we have that

$$\alpha\bar{\alpha}=|\alpha|^2. \tag{1.9}$$

We remark once more that $|\alpha|=0$ if and only if $\alpha=0$ and that for all complex numbers, other than zero, $|\alpha|>0$. Of course, different complex numbers may have the same

† We adopt the convention that the square root of a non-negative real number always stands for the positive square root.

modulus, for example, conjugate complex numbers always have the same modulus, thus $|\alpha|=|\bar{\alpha}|$. Again, if $\alpha=\cos\theta+i\sin\theta$, where θ is an arbitrary real number, then $|\alpha|=\sqrt{(\cos^2\theta+\sin^2\theta)}=1$. When $\alpha=a$ is real, the definition (1.8) reduces to $\alpha=\sqrt{a^2}$, which is equal to a if $a>0$ and is equal to $-a$ if $a<0$. This agrees with the definition of the modulus $|a|$ of a real number a, which is therefore generalized by (1.8).

Let $\beta=c+id$ be another complex number. We want to consider the modulus of the product $\alpha\beta$. Using (1.7) and (1.9) we find that

$$|\alpha\beta|^2=(\alpha\beta)(\overline{\alpha\beta})=\alpha\beta\bar{\alpha}\bar{\beta}=\alpha\bar{\alpha}\beta\bar{\beta}=|\alpha|^2|\beta|^2. \qquad (1.10)$$

Since the moduli are never negative the extraction of the square roots introduces no ambiguity, and we arrive at the very simple result that

$$|\alpha\beta|=|\alpha|\,|\beta|. \qquad (1.11)$$

When we wish to translate this result into a statement about real numbers, we work out $|\alpha\beta|$ by substituting in (1.8) the values for $\mathscr{R}(\alpha\beta)$ and $\mathscr{I}(\alpha\beta)$ from (1.5), thus

$$|\alpha\beta|^2=(ac-bd)^2+(ad+bc)^2.$$

Hence (1.10) is equivalent to the interesting identity

$$(ac-bd)^2+(ad+bc)^2=(a^2+b^2)(c^2+d^2),$$

which of course could be readily verified by direct calculation. In particular, when $\alpha=\beta$, the multiplication formula (1.11) becomes $|\alpha^2|=|\alpha|^2$, and by repeating this argument we find that $|\alpha^n|=|\alpha|^n$, where n is any positive integer.

Examples.

$$|i|=|-i|=1,\ |-5|=5.\ |1+i|=\sqrt{(1^2+1^2)}=\sqrt{2}.$$
$$|(1+i)^4|=4.\ |\tan\theta+i|=\sqrt{\{(\tan\theta)^2+1^2\}}=|\sec\theta|.$$

We can now describe a simple solution to the problem of division. Let $\alpha=a+ib$ and $\beta=c+id$ be given complex numbers and suppose that $\alpha\neq0$. It is required to find a number $\xi=x+iy$ such that

$$\alpha\xi=\beta\ (\alpha\neq0) \qquad (1.12)$$

8

Let us assume for a moment that there exists such a number ξ. Then on multiplying (1.12) by α we find that $\alpha\bar{\alpha}\,\xi = \bar{\alpha}\beta$, that is

$$(a^2+b^2)(x+iy) = (a-ib)(c+id) = (ac+bd)+i(ad-bc).$$

On comparing real and imaginary parts on both sides we see that

$$x = \frac{ac+bd}{a^2+b^2}, \quad y = \frac{ad-bc}{a^2+b^2}.$$

Thus if there is a solution at all, it must be given by

$$\xi = \frac{ac+bd}{a^2+b^2} + i\frac{ad-bc}{a^2+b^2} = \frac{1}{|\alpha|^2}\bar{\alpha}\beta. \tag{1.13}$$

Conversely, it is easy to see that (1.13) does in fact satisfy (1.12). Indeed, $\alpha\dfrac{1}{|\alpha|^2}\bar{\alpha}\beta = \dfrac{\alpha\bar{\alpha}}{|\alpha|^2}\beta = \beta$. The unique solution, exhibited in (1.13), will be written β/α or $\beta\alpha^{-1}$, or $\alpha^{-1}\beta$. There is no need to memorize the explicit formula for β/α. The argument which shows that there is such a complex number is equivalent to the familiar 'rationalization of denominators' in working with surds. Indeed, it should be borne in mind that, after all, $i = \sqrt{-1}$ is a surd. To simplify a complex fraction we multiply numerator and denominator by the conjugate complex of the denominator, thus

$$\frac{c+id}{a+ib} = \frac{(c+id)(a-ib)}{(a+ib)(a-ib)} = \frac{(ac+bd)+i(ad-bc)}{a^2+b^2}, \tag{1.14}$$

which is equivalent to (1.13). In particular, we note that if $\alpha \neq 0$,

$$\frac{1}{\alpha} = \frac{\bar{\alpha}}{|\alpha|^2} = \frac{a-ib}{a^2+b^2}, \quad \left|\frac{1}{\alpha}\right| = \frac{1}{|\alpha|}. \tag{1.15}$$

Summarizing, we can say that complex numbers are mathematical objects for which addition, subtraction, subtraction and division are defined in such a way that the seven fundamental laws are satisfied. The real numbers may be regarded as particular cases of complex numbers, so that any general property of complex numbers also holds for real numbers. However, the converse of this statement is not true. For example, there is no simple order relation between complex numbers and the symbol $\alpha < \beta$ is not defined, nor is there any sense in referring to a complex number as being positive or negative. These are attributes of real numbers which cannot be transferred to complex numbers.

The simplest type of problem consists in reducing an expression involving complex numbers to its standard form, that is to the form $x + iy$, where x and y are real. This will be illustrated in the following examples.

Example 1.

$$\frac{(1+2i)^2}{1-i} = \frac{1+4i+4i^2}{1-i} = \frac{-3+4i}{1-i} = \frac{(-3+4i)(1+i)}{(1-i)(1+i)}$$
$$= \frac{-7+i}{2} = -\frac{7}{2} + \frac{1}{2}i.$$

Example 2.

$$\frac{1}{1+i} + \frac{1}{1-2i} = \frac{1-i}{(1+i)(1-i)} + \frac{1+2i}{(1-2i)(1+2i)}$$
$$= \frac{1-i}{2} + \frac{1+2i}{5} = \frac{7}{10} - \frac{1}{10}i.$$

Example 3.

$$1 + i + i^2 + i^3 + i^4 + i^5 + i^6 + i^7 = \frac{1-i^8}{1-i} = \frac{1-(i^4)^2}{1-i} = 0.$$

Let $f(x) = a_0 x^n + a_1 x^{n-1} + \ldots + a_{n-1} x + a_n$ be a polynominal with real coefficients $a_0, a_1, a_2, \ldots, a_n$. If we substitute for x a complex number α, we obtain the number

$$f(\alpha) = a_0 \alpha^n + a_1 \alpha^{n-1} + a_2 \alpha^{n-2} + \ldots + a_{n-1} \alpha + a_n. \quad (1.16)$$

We now wish to find $f(\bar{\alpha})$. By a repeated application of (1.6) and (1.7) we may do this by placing a bar across each term on the right-hand side of (1.16) and across all the factors of this term. But since the coefficients are real $\bar{a}_0 = a_0$,

10

THE ALGEBRAIC THEORY

$\bar{a}_1 = a_1,$ . . . Hence $\overline{f(\alpha)} = a_0(\bar{\alpha})^n + a_1(\bar{\alpha})^{n-1} + \ldots + a_n.$ Or, briefly,

$$\overline{f(\alpha)} = f(\bar{\alpha}). \qquad (1.17)$$

Suppose now that $f(\alpha) = 0$. Then also $\overline{f(\alpha)} = 0$ and (1.17) implies that $f(\bar{\alpha}) = 0$. Thus we have proved the important result that *if $f(x) = 0$ is an equation with real coefficients, its roots are either real numbers or occur in pairs of conjugate complex numbers $\alpha, \bar{\alpha}$.*

We have so far confined ourselves to the four rules of arithmetic for complex numbers. A systematic study of more complicated functions will be deferred until geometrical and analytical ideas have been introduced into the subject. However, the extraction of square roots is an elementary process which can be discussed already at this stage.

Let $\alpha = a + ib$ be a given complex number. It is required to find a number $\xi = x + iy$ such that $\xi^2 = \alpha$, that is

$$(x + iy)^2 = a + ib.$$

On splitting this equation into real and imaginary components, we have that

$$x^2 - y^2 = a, \quad 2xy = b. \qquad (1.18)$$

Suppose first that such a number ξ exists. By taking moduli, we deduce that $|\alpha| = |\xi^2| = |\xi|^2$, whence on squaring $(|\xi|^2)^2 = |\alpha|^2$, that is

$$(x^2 + y^2)^2 = a^2 + b^2. \qquad (1.19)$$

Combining this with (1.18) we find that

$$x^2 = \tfrac{1}{2}(a + \sqrt{(a^2 + b^2)}), \quad y^2 = \tfrac{1}{2}(-a + \sqrt{(a^2 + b^2)}).$$

The expressions on the right-hand sides of these equations are never negative, so that the extraction of the square roots yield real values for x and y, as it should. But when choosing the alternative signs for x and y it must be remembered that $xy = \tfrac{1}{2}b$. Thus when b is positive, x and y have the same sign, and when b is negative, they have the opposite sign. There are therefore exactly two, and not four solutions of the equation $\xi^2 = \alpha$ ($\alpha \neq 0$), as one would expect: if

11

ALGEBRAIC THEORY OF COMPLEX NUMBERS

$\xi_1 = x_1 + iy_1$ is one solution, then the other solution is $\xi_2 = -\xi_1 = -x_1 - iy_1$. In a numerical problem it is usually best to find the value of one of the unknowns, say x, and then to obtain the other from the equation $xy = \frac{1}{2}b$.

Example. Evaluate $\sqrt{(5-12i)}$. Let $\sqrt{(5-12i)} = x+iy$. Then $x^2 - y^2 = 5$, $2xy = -12$. By (1.19), $x^2 + y^2 = \sqrt{(5^2 + (-12)^2)}$, $x^2 + y^2 = \sqrt{169} = 13$, with no ambiguity of sign, since $x^2 + y^2 > 0$. It now follows that $2x^2 = 5 + 13 = 18$, $x = \pm 3$, $y = -6/x = \mp 2$. Thus $\sqrt{(5-12i)} = \pm(3-2i)$.

The reader will recall that the number i was originally introduced in order to ensure the solubility of certain quadratic equations with real coefficients. At first sight it might be suspected that the solution of quadratic equations with complex coefficients might require still more general numbers. However, this is not so. In fact, the roots of
$$\alpha\xi^2 + \beta\xi + \gamma = 0,$$
where $\alpha(\neq 0)$, β, γ are complex numbers, are still given by the formula
$$(1/2\alpha)\{-\beta \pm \sqrt{(\beta^2 - 4\alpha\gamma)}\}. \tag{1.20}$$

It is true, the expression under the square root is now in general a complex number, but we know that the square root of a complex number is again a complex number and not a number of a higher type.

EXERCISES ON CHAPTER ONE

1. Express in the form $x+iy$, where x and y are real,
   (i) $(1+2i)(3+4i)$, (ii) $\dfrac{1}{3+2i}$, (iii) $(2+i)^4$, (iv) $\dfrac{1}{(4+2i)(2-3i)}$,
   (v) $\dfrac{3+4i}{1+2i}$, (vi) $\dfrac{1-i}{1+i}$.
2. Solve for ξ:
   (i) $(2+i)\xi + i = 3$.
   (ii) $\dfrac{\xi-1}{\xi-i} = \dfrac{2}{3}$.
3. Find the sum to n terms
   $i + (2+3i) + (4+5i) + (6+7i) + \ldots + \{2n-2 + (2n-1)i\}$.

THE ALGEBRAIC THEORY

4. Find the modulus of (i) $4+3i$, (ii) $(2-i)^6$, (iii) $\dfrac{1}{5+12i}$,

   (iv) $\dfrac{1+2it-t^2}{1+t^2}$ (t real).

5. Show that $\left|\dfrac{\alpha}{\beta}\right|=\dfrac{|\alpha|}{|\beta|}$. Find the modulus of $\dfrac{(1+2i)^{12}}{(1-2i)^9}$.

6. Evaluate (i) $\sqrt{i}$, (ii) $(2+2i)^{\frac{1}{2}}$, (iii) $(3+4i)^{\frac{1}{2}}$.

7. Solve the equation $\xi^2-(3+i)\xi+4+3i=0$.

8. Find a quadratic with real coefficients which has $2+i$ as one of its roots. What is the other root?

9. Prove that $|\alpha+\beta|^2+|\alpha-\beta|^2=2|\alpha|^2+2|\beta|^2$.

10. Solve $z^4-2z^2+4=0$.

CHAPTER TWO
Geometrical Representations

We have already remarked that the complex number $x+iy$ may be thought of as an ordered pair (x, y) of real numbers. As the reader knows from co-ordinate geometry, such a pair of real numbers may be regarded as the co-ordinates of a point in a plane. We are thus led to the following geometrical interpretation of complex numbers: choose a plane and furnish it with Cartesian rectangular axes Ox, Oy. Let the number $x+iy$ be represented by the point $P=(x, y)$. In this way we can plot complex numbers as points of a plane (see Fig. 2). This plane (or more correctly

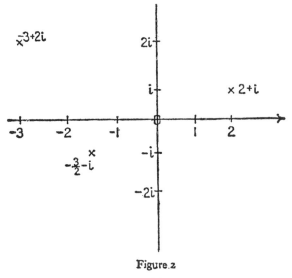

Figure.2

such a plane) is often called the *Argand plane* or *Argand diagram* or simply the *complex plane*. Any algebraical proposition between complex numbers can be translated into a geometrical relation between the corresponding points of the Argand plane, and conversely, any relation between points of a plane can, in principle, be regarded as a relation between complex numbers. The reader should, however, keep the logical situation clearly in mind: we have defined complex numbers as algebraical objects obeying certain laws of composition. The points of the Argand plane afford a pictorial representation, which is helpful for many theoretical and practical purposes. But the representation must not be confused with the object itself. By way of analogy, temperature is often represented by the height of a column of mercury, and this is a very useful device. But nobody would suggest that temperature is a column of mercury. Besides there are other ways of representing complex numbers (and temperature).

From now on we shall frequently use the traditional notation for a complex number by means of a single Latin letter, thus $z = x + iy$ or $w = u + iv$, where x, y, u and v are real. For the sake of brevity, we often speak of 'the point z', when we should say 'the point representing z'. Since the x-axis consists of all the real points, it is called the *real axis*. Similarly, the y-axis contains all the purely imaginary points. It is, somewhat misleadingly, called the *imaginary axis*. (It is, of course, no more imaginary than the real axis.) The origin O corresponds to the number zero.

A different, but related interpretation of complex numbers is obtained, if we associate with the complex number $x + iy$ the vector $\overrightarrow{OP}$, where $P = (x, y)$, or more generally, by the directed segment $\overrightarrow{P_1 P_2}$, where $P_1 = (x_1, y_1)$, $P_2 = (x_2, y_2)$ and $x_2 - x_1 = x$, $y_2 - y_1 = y$. Again, if no misunderstanding can arise, we speak of the vector z instead of the vector representing z, and we shall even commit the convenient abuse of language by writing $z = \overrightarrow{OP}$.

15

Let us translate the formula for the sum of z and w into vector language, where $z=x+iy$ and $w=u+iv$. We represent z and w by the vectors $\overrightarrow{OP}$ and $\overrightarrow{OQ}$ respectively (see Fig. 3).

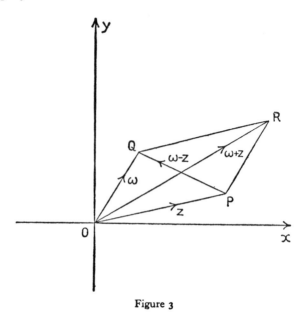

Figure 3

Then $z+w=(x+u)+i(y+v)$ corresponds to the vector $\overrightarrow{OR}$, where $R=(x+u,\ y+v)$. Evidently R is the fourth vertex of the parallelogram, the other three vertices of which are Q, O and P. Thus we have verified that the addition of complex numbers obeys the parallelogram law. Note that z and w may equally well be represented by $\overrightarrow{QR}$ and $\overrightarrow{PR}$ respectively. We then have the relations

$$\overrightarrow{OR}=\overrightarrow{OP}+\overrightarrow{PR} \text{ and } \overrightarrow{OR}=\overrightarrow{OQ}+\overrightarrow{QR},$$

16

either of which may be described as the triangle law of addition. The geometrical relation

$$\overrightarrow{OP} + \overrightarrow{PR} = \overrightarrow{OQ} + \overrightarrow{QR} \ (= \overrightarrow{OR})$$

means that $z + w = w + z$, confirming the commutative law of addition. In order to represent the sum $w = z_1 + z_2 + \ldots + z_n$ of several complex numbers we fit the vectors that correspond to $z_1, z_2, \ldots, z_n$ into a broken line starting from O (see Fig. 4).

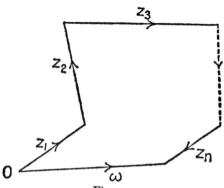

Figure 4

$P_1, P_2, P_3, \ldots$ are the points at the ends of $z_1, z_2, z_3, \ldots$

The vector that joins O to the end point of the vector z_n then corresponds to w. In particular, the relation $z_1 + z_2 + \ldots + z_n = 0$ means that the broken line $OP_1P_2 \ldots P_n$ is a closed polygon ($O = P_n$).

The difference between two complex numbers can also be simply represented by the vector diagram. If $\overrightarrow{OP}$ and $\overrightarrow{OQ}$ correspond to z and w respectively, then $w - z$ is represented by $\overrightarrow{PQ}$, that is by the vector that joins the end point of z to the end point of w.

If z is represented by the vector $\overrightarrow{OP}$, where $P = (x, y)$, then the length of this vector is given by

$$|z| = \sqrt{(x^2 + y^2)}.$$

17

More generally, if z is represented by $\overrightarrow{P_1 P_2}$, then $|z| = P_1 P_2$, the length of the segment $P_1 P_2$. For let $\overrightarrow{OP_1} = z_1 = x_1 + iy_1$, $\overrightarrow{OP_2} = x_2 + iy_2$, $z = z_2 - z_1$. Then $|z|^2 = (x_2 - x_1)^2 + (y_2 - y_1)^2$, that is $|z| = P_1 P_2$, the length of the segment.

If λ is real, the vector λz is parallel to the vector z and its length is λ times that of z. If $\lambda > 0$, the vectors z and λz have the same direction, whilst if $\lambda < 0$, their directions are opposite to each other (see Fig. 5, where $\lambda > 1$). In particular, note that $|-z| = |z|$. If $z \neq 0$, the vector $\dfrac{1}{|z|} z$ is a unit vector (that is a vector of unit length) and has the same direction as z.

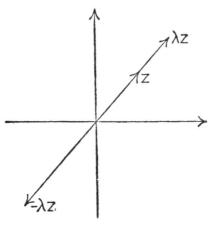

Figure 5

Consider again the triangle OPR (Fig. 3) which illustrates the formula $z + w = w + z$. Using the Euclidean proposition that the sum of two sides in a triangle cannot be less than a third, we arrive at the important 'triangle inequality'

$$|z + w| \leqslant |z| + |w|. \qquad (2.1)$$

18

The reader will understand that this is an inequality between the moduli of complex numbers and not between the complex numbers themselves (as we know there is no such thing). The equality sign in (2.1) holds if and only if the triangle OPR collapses, that is if $w = \lambda z$, where λ is a positive (real) number.

By a repeated application of (2.1) we obtain the more general inequality

$$|z_1 + z_2 + \ldots + z_n| \leqslant |z_1| + |z_2| + \ldots + |z_n|.$$

It must not be supposed that there is an analogous inequality for $|z - w|$ with the inequality going the other way. Indeed, since $|-w| = |w|$, we can assert only that

$$|z - w| = |z + (-w)| \leqslant |z| + |w|.$$

A more useful deduction from (2.1) is as follows: put $z = z_2$ and $w = z_1 - z_2$, so that $z + w = z_1$. Then (2.1) becomes

$$|z_1| \leqslant |z_2| + |z_1 - z_2|,$$

or

$$|z_1 - z_2| \geqslant |z_1| - |z_2|. \tag{2.2}$$

Now it is clear that by a suitable choice of z and w we can make z_1 and z_2 equal to any two preassigned complex numbers. In particular, (2.2) holds for the pair (z_2, z_1) in which z_1 and z_2 are interchanged. Thus we also have that

$$|z_2 - z_1| \geqslant |z_2| - |z_1|.$$

On the other hand, $|z_2 - z_1| = |-(z_1 - z_2)| = |z_1 - z_2|$, so that, as a companion result to (2.2),

$$|z_1 - z_2| \geqslant |z_2| - |z_1|. \tag{2.3}$$

One of the inequalities (2.2) or (2.3) is trivial since its right-hand side is negative or zero. Choosing whichever gives a significant result we can write

$$|z_1 - z_2| \geqslant \left| |z_1| - |z_2| \right|, \tag{2.4}$$

which is valid in all cases.

A variable complex number z (or a *complex variable*, as we shall henceforth say) which is subject to one or more

19

conditions traces out a part of the complex plane. Very often such conditions involve the modulus of complex numbers.

Example 1. The equation $|z-a|=r$ where r is positive,† describes the circle with radius r and centre at a. The interior of the circle is represented by $|z-a|<r$ and the exterior by $|z-a|>r$.

Example 2. The relation $\mathcal{R}z>\lambda$ (λ real) states that z lies in the half-plane to the right of the vertical line $x=\lambda$.

Example 3. Suppose z is restricted by the condition

$$|z-1|=|z+1|. \tag{2.5}$$

Since, generally, $|z-a|$ gives the distance between z and a, equation (2.5) corresponds to the locus of points equidistant from 1 and -1, which clearly is the imaginary axis (y-axis), that is $\mathcal{R}z=0$ (see Fig. 6).

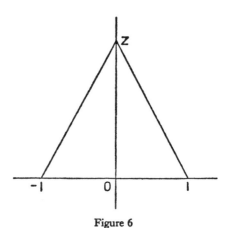

Figure 6

Alternatively, we can obtain the result by calculation.

† We make the convention that the terms positive and negative shall imply that the number in question is real.

Thus on squaring (2.5) we find that

$$|z-1|^2 = |z+1|^2,$$
$$(z-1)(\bar{z}-1) = (z+1)(\bar{z}+1),$$

whence on expanding and simplifying, $2(z+\bar{z})=0$, that is $\mathscr{R}z=0$.

Example 4. A line which does not pass through the origin, may be represented by an equation of the form

$$\mathscr{R}(az)=1 \qquad (2.6)$$

where a is a suitable complex number. Indeed, let $a=l-im$. Then (2.6) is readily found to be equivalent to $lx+my=1$, the familiar equation of a straight line which does not pass through the origin.

In order to discuss the geometrical interpretation of the product of complex numbers it is convenient to use polar co-ordinates (r, θ) rather than Cartesian co-ordinates (x, y). The reader is no doubt familiar with the equations

$$x=r \cos \theta$$
$$y=r \sin \theta, \qquad (2.7)$$

which express the relations between these two systems of co-ordinates (Fig. 7).

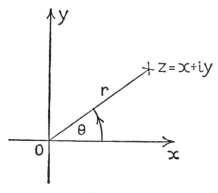

Figure 7

21

Note that
$$r=\sqrt{(x^2+y^2)}=|z|, \tag{2.8}$$

which immediately gives us a geometrical interpretation of the modulus: $|z|$ is the distance of the point z from the origin. The angle θ will always be measured in radians, unless the contrary is stated. Its value is, however, not completely determined by the equations (2.7), since arbitrary whole multiples of 2π can evidently be added or subtracted from it. In order to obviate this ambiguity, we impose the further condition that

$$-\pi<\theta\leqslant\pi. \tag{2.9}$$

For a given non-zero number z there exists one and only one value of θ which satisfies (2.7) and (2.9). This value is called the *argument* of z, and we write

$$\theta=\text{arg } z. \tag{2.10}$$

We do not define arg 0. The relation $\tan\theta=y/x$, which is an immediate consequence of (2.7), does not determine θ uniquely, if, as is customary the function $\tan^{-1}t$ is defined in such a way that, for all t,
$$-\tfrac{1}{2}\pi\leqslant\tan^{-1}t\leqslant\tfrac{1}{2}\pi.$$
Generally, the value of $\tan^{-1}(y/x)$ is equal either to θ or to $\theta+\pi$ or to $\theta-\pi$, and it is only after examining the signs of both x and y and observing the condition (2.9) that we can decide which of these three values is the correct one.

Examples.

(i) arg $3=0$, (ii) arg $(-3)=\pi$, (iii) arg $(1+i)=\pi/4$, (iv) arg $(-1-i)=-\pi/4$. (Note that in both (iii) and (iv) $\tan^{-1}(y/x)=\pi/4$.), (v) arg $2i=\tfrac{1}{2}\pi$, (vi) arg $(-i)=-\tfrac{1}{2}\pi$.

In virtue of (2.7) the complex number $z=x+iy$ can now be written in what we shall call the *polar form*, that is

$$z=r(\cos\theta+i\sin\theta) \tag{2.11}$$

where $r=|z|$ and $\theta=\text{arg } z$. Conversely, if z has been expressed in the form (2.11), where r and θ are real and satisfy the inequalities $r \geqslant 0$, and $-\pi < \theta \leqslant \pi$, then this is the polar form of z, that is we may infer that $r=|z|$ and $\theta = \arg z$.

Next, consider two complex numbers in polar form,
$$z_1 = r_1(\cos \theta_1 + i \sin \theta_1), \quad z_2 = r_2(\cos \theta_2 + i \sin \theta_2).$$
We then have $z_1 z_2 = r_1 r_2 (\cos \theta_1 + i \sin \theta_1)(\cos \theta_2 + i \sin \theta_2)$
$= r_1 r_2 \{(\cos \theta_1 \cos \theta_2 - \sin \theta_1 \sin \theta_2) + i(\sin \theta_1 \cos \theta_2 + \cos \theta_1 \sin \theta_2)\}$ so that
$$z_1 z_2 = r_1 r_2 \{\cos (\theta_1 + \theta_2) + i \sin (\theta_1 + \theta_2)\}. \qquad (2.12)$$
From this equation we immediately deduce the fact, already known to us, that
$$|z_1 z_2| = r_1 r_2 = |z_1| \, |z_2|.$$
On the other hand, it would not be correct to say that $\arg z_1 z_2$ is equal to $\theta_1 + \theta_2$, because this number might fall outside the range (2.9). All we can assert is that
$$\arg (z_1 z_2) = \arg z_1 + \arg z_2 + 2k\pi, \qquad (2.13)$$
where $k = 0$ or 1 or -1, and it is only on examining condition (2.9) that we can decide which is the correct value of k.

If z has the polar form (2.11), then
$$\bar{z} = r(\cos \theta - i \sin \theta) = r\{\cos (-\theta) + i \sin (-\theta)\}.$$
When $z \neq 0$, we can use (1.15), that is $z^{-1} = r^{-2}\bar{z}$. Hence
$$\frac{1}{z} = \frac{1}{r} (\cos \theta - i \sin \theta). \qquad (2.14)$$
It follows that
$$\arg \bar{z} = \arg \frac{1}{z} = - \arg z,$$
unless z is a real negative number. When this is the case, say when $x = -p$, where p is positive, then $\arg (-p) = \arg \left(-\dfrac{1}{p}\right) = \pi$. By combining (2.14) with (2.12) we can easily obtain a formula for the quotient of two complex numbers. Using the same notation as before and assuming that $z_2 \neq 0$, we find that
$$\frac{z_1}{z_2} = z_1 \frac{1}{z_2} = \frac{r_1}{r_2}(\cos \theta_1 + i \sin \theta_1)(\cos (-\theta_2) + i \sin (-\theta_2)).$$

Thus

$$\frac{z_1}{z_2}=\frac{r_1}{r_2}\{\cos(\theta_1-\theta_2)+i\sin(\theta_1-\theta_2)\}$$

is the polar form of z_1/z_2. We may therefore infer that (i) $|z_1/z_2|=r_1/r_2$ and (ii) $\arg(z_1/z_2)=\arg z_1-\arg z_2+2k\pi$, where $k=0$ or 1 or -1. If we are interested only in the lines along which the vectors z_1 and z_2 lie and not in the sense of their direction, then it may be stated that $\arg(z_1/z_2)$ determines the angle between these lines.

Let us apply the product formula to the special case in which one of the factors is i. Since $|i|=1$ and $\arg i=\frac{1}{2}\pi$, the polar form of i is $i=\cos\frac{1}{2}\pi+i\sin\frac{1}{2}\pi$. Hence

$$zi=r\{\cos(\theta+\tfrac{1}{2}\pi)+i\sin(\theta+\tfrac{1}{2}\pi)\}.$$

Thus the vector zi is obtained from the vector z by a rotation through $\frac{1}{2}\pi$. On repeating this operation we shall have rotated z through π, that is into the vector $-z$, or in symbols, $((z)i)i=-z$. This affords a geometrical illustration of the fact that $i^2=-1$.

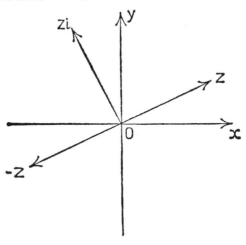

Figure 8

More generally, if a is a fixed non-zero complex number and z is a complex variable, we may interpret the product az (or za) as an operation to be performed on z, that is the vector z is carried into the vector az. If $a = \rho\,(\cos\alpha + i\sin\alpha)$ the operation $z \to az$ amounts to multiplying the length of the vector z by ρ and rotating its direction through an angle α.

Example 1. *Prove that the diagonals of a rhombus intersect at right angles.* We may represent the vertices of the rhombus by the numbers 0, a and b, subject to the conditions

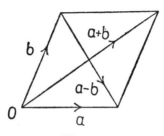

Figure 9

that $|a| = |b| \neq 0$ and $a \neq \pm b$ (see Fig. 9). The diagonals are then represented by $a - b$ and $a + b$ respectively. Our geometrical proposition amounts to the assertion that $\arg (a-b)/(a+b) = \pm\,\pi/2$, or, in other words, that $q = (a-b)/(a+b)$ is a purely imaginary number. The necessary and sufficient condition for this is that $q + \bar{q} = 0$. Indeed we readily find that

$$q + \bar{q} = \frac{a-b}{a+b} + \frac{\bar{a} - \bar{b}}{\bar{a} + \bar{b}} = \frac{2a\bar{a} - 2b\bar{b}}{(a+b)(\bar{a} + \bar{b})} = 0,$$

because $|a| = |b|$.

Example 2. The distinct points z_1, z_2 and z_3 are collinear if and only if

25

$$\frac{z_1 - z_3}{z_3 - z_2} = \lambda$$

is real, and then z_3 divides the segment represented by $z_1 - z_2$ in the ratio λ, with the understanding that $\lambda > 0$, if z_3 in an internal point and that $\lambda < 0$ if z_3 is an external point of subdivision. The condition is equivalent to the statement that the vector $z_1 - z_3$ is a real multiple of the vector $z_3 - z_2$ so that both lie in the same line.

Note that if z_3 is the mid-point of z_1 and z_2, then $\lambda = 1$ and therefore $z_3 = \frac{1}{2}(z_1 + z_2)$.

Example 3. Let a and b be fixed complex numbers ánd let z be a variable, representing the points A, B and Z respectively. Then the equation

$$\arg \frac{z - b}{z - a} = \lambda,$$

where λ is a real constant satisfying $-\pi < \lambda \leqslant \pi$, represents the circular arc that has AB as a chord subtending an

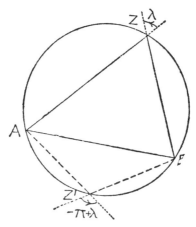

Figure 10

26

angle λ at a point Z of the circumference. The complementary arc $\overset{\frown}{AZ'B}$ is described by the equation

$$\arg \frac{z'-b}{z'-a} = -\pi+\lambda$$

(see Fig. 10).

We now return to the multiplication formula (2.12), which we generalize as follows. Let $z_1, z_2, \ldots, z_n$ be a set of complex numbers, each presented in polar form, say

$$z_k = r_k(\cos \theta_k + i \sin \theta_k) \ (k=1, 2, \ldots, n).$$

By a repeated application of (2.12) we find that the product of these numbers is given by

$$z_1 z_2 \ldots z_n =$$
$$r_1 r_2 \ldots r_n \{\cos (\theta_1+\theta_2+\ldots+\theta_n) + i \sin (\theta_1+\theta_2+\ldots+\theta_n)\}.$$

In particular, when $z_1=z_2=\ldots=z_n=z$, we deduce that

$$z^n = r^n(\cos n\theta + i \sin n\theta). \tag{2.15}$$

Specializing still further let us take a number z for which $r=1$, thus $z=\cos \theta + i \sin \theta$. Equation (2.15) then becomes

$$(\cos \theta + i \sin \theta)^n = \cos n\theta + i \sin n\theta \tag{2.16}$$

This remarkable formula is known as *de Moivre's Theorem.* We have so far proved it only when n is a positive integer. The formula is evidently true when $n=0$, if as is usual we equate z^0 to 1. Next, let n be a negative integer, say $n=-q$, where $q>0$. Then

$$(\cos \theta + i \sin \theta)^n = [(\cos \theta + i \sin \theta)^q]^{-1} = [\cos q\theta + i \sin q\theta]^{-1}$$
$$= \cos(-q\theta) + i \sin(-q\theta) \text{ by } (2.14)$$
$$= \cos n\theta + i \sin n\theta,$$

which establishes the validity of (2.16) for negative n.

Summarizing we can say that the nth power of the function $\cos \theta + i \sin \theta$ may be obtained simply by multiplying the argument θ by n. The reader will know this phenomenon from the general exponential function. For let $f(x)=a^{\gamma x}$, where a and γ are constants and a is positive. Then, evidently, $[f(x)]^n = f(nx)$. We shall now demonstrate that $\cos \theta + i \sin \theta$ is in fact an exponential function of a special kind, and it is only with this knowledge that we can gain a real understanding of de Moivre's striking but seemingly mysterious discovery.

At this point we have to anticipate some results that will be systematically treated in Chapter Four (p. 43). When z is a complex number, the function e^z (or exp z, as it is more conveniently, but more clumsily printed) is defined by the infinite series

$$e^z = \exp z = 1 + \frac{z}{1!} + \frac{z^2}{2!} + \frac{z^3}{3!} + \ldots + \frac{z^n}{n!} + \ldots \quad (2.17)$$

When $z = x$ is real, this series reduces to the well-known formula† for e^x. We will not stop here to give an exact explanation of what is meant by an infinite series with complex terms, and we ask the reader to take it on trust that the function defined by (2.17) has the properties expected of it. In particular,

$$\exp(z_1 + z_2 + \ldots + z_m) = \exp z_1 \exp z_2 \ldots \exp z_m$$

whence $\exp(mz) = (\exp z)^m$. Let us now put $z = i\theta$, where θ is real. We then obtain that

$$e^{i\theta} = 1 + \frac{i\theta}{1!} + \frac{(i\theta)^2}{2!} + \frac{(i\theta)^3}{3!} + \frac{(i\theta)^4}{4!} + \ldots + \frac{(i\theta)^n}{n!} + \ldots$$

$$= \left(1 - \frac{\theta^2}{2!} + \frac{\theta^4}{4!} - \frac{\theta^6}{6!} + \ldots\right) + i\left(\theta - \frac{\theta^3}{3!} + \frac{\theta^5}{5!} - \frac{\theta^7}{7!} + \ldots\right),$$

the rearrangement of terms being easily justified by an appeal to general results in the theory of convergence (see p. 52). If we now use the familiar series‡

$$\cos\theta = 1 - \frac{\theta^2}{2!} + \frac{\theta^4}{4!} - \ldots, \quad \sin\theta = \theta - \frac{\theta^3}{3!} + \frac{\theta^5}{5!} - \ldots$$

for real θ, we find that

$$e^{i\theta} = \cos\theta + i\sin\theta. \quad (2.18)$$

From the general property of the exponential function it is now clear that $(\exp i\theta)^m = \exp im\theta$, that is $(\cos\theta + i\sin\theta)^m = \cos m\theta + i\sin m\theta$, and we have not only proved de Moivre's theorem once more but have at the same time placed it into the right setting.

† P. J. Hilton, *Differential Calculus*, p. 27.　　‡ *Ibid.*, p. 44.

The result (2.18) is known as *Euler's formula*. It is one of the most surprising discoveries in mathematics. By extending our number system to include the complex numbers we find that the trigonometric functions $\cos \theta$ and $\sin \theta$ are intimately related to the exponential function. This fact alone would surely justify the introduction of complex numbers. Let us consider a few special cases:

$$e^{i\pi/4} = \cos\frac{\pi}{4} + i \sin\frac{\pi}{4} = (1+i)/\sqrt{2}.$$

$$e^{i\pi/2} = \cos \tfrac{1}{2}\pi + i \sin \tfrac{1}{2}\pi = i, \; e^{-i\pi/2} = -i,$$

$$e^{i\pi} = \cos \pi + i \sin \pi = -1, \; e^{-i\pi} = -1, \text{ and finally,}$$

$$e^{2i\pi} = 1. \tag{2.19}$$

This last result has far-reaching consequences. For if z is any complex number, it follows that

$$\exp(z+2\pi i) = \exp z \exp 2\pi i = \exp z. \tag{2.20}$$

Thus the value of the exponential function remains unaltered when the variable z is augmented by $2\pi i$. More generally, (2.19) can be replaced by $\exp(2mi\pi)=1$ and (2.20) by

$$\exp(z+2m\pi i) = \exp z \; (m=0, \pm 1, \pm 2, \ldots) \tag{2.21}$$

We shall later see (p. 53) that if $\exp(z+p)=\exp z$ for all z, then $p=2k\pi i$, where k is an integer. The equation (2.20) is related to, and indeed a consequence of, the familiar fact that $\cos \theta$ and $\sin \theta$ are periodic functions with period 2π, that is $\cos(\theta+2\pi)=\cos \theta$ and $\sin(\theta+2\pi)=\sin \theta$ for all θ. By analogy we shall now say that e^z, too, is a periodic function, whose period is $2\pi i$, a purely imaginary number. The periodicity of the exponential function remains hidden, if we restrict the variable to real values. It is important to observe that when complex numbers are involved, the equation $\exp z_1 = \exp z_2$ does not necessarily imply that $z_1 = z_2$, but only that $z_1 = z_2 + 2\pi i k$, where k is an integer.

The polar form of a complex number may now be written more concisely as

$$z = r\,e^{i\theta}.$$

Equation (2.18) tells us that in certain cases the exponential function can be expressed in terms of the trigonometric functions. We shall now show that, conversely, the trigonometric functions can be reduced to simple combinations of exponential functions. For since the value of θ in (2.18) was quite arbitrary, we may replace θ by $-\theta$. Thus together with (2.18) we have that

$$e^{-i\theta} = \cos\theta - i\sin\theta.$$

Solving these two equations with respect to $\sin\theta$ and $\cos\theta$ we obtain that

$$\cos\theta = \tfrac{1}{2}(e^{i\theta} + e^{-i\theta}), \quad \sin\theta = \frac{1}{2i}(e^{i\theta} - e^{-i\theta}) \qquad (2.22)$$

We have derived these equations only for real θ. But we shall later see that they are in fact valid for complex values of the variable (p. 54).

As a further illustration we discuss the use of complex numbers in the summation of certain trigonometric series.

Example 1. Find a simple formula for the sum

$$C = \cos(\alpha + \theta) + \cos(\alpha + 2\theta) + \ldots + \cos(\alpha + n\theta), \qquad (2.23)$$

where α and θ are arbitrary real numbers, except that $\theta \neq 2\pi k$ (k an integer). Along with (2.23) consider the sum

$$S = \sin(\alpha + \theta) + \sin(\alpha + 2\theta) + \ldots + \sin(\alpha + n\theta).$$

By Euler's formula (2.18), $\cos(\alpha + r\theta) + i\sin(\alpha + r\theta) = e^{(\alpha + r\theta)}$, so that

$$C + i\,S = \sum_{r=1}^{n} e^{i(\alpha + r\theta)} = e^{i\alpha}\sum_{r=1}^{n} e^{ir\theta}.$$

The last sum is a finite geometric progression with ratio $e^{i\theta}$. Thus

30

$$C+i\,S=e^{i\alpha}\,e^{i\theta}\,\frac{e^{in\theta}-1}{e^{i\theta}-1}=e^{i\alpha+\frac{n+1}{2}i\theta}\,\frac{e^{in\theta/2}-e^{-in\theta/2}}{e^{i\theta/2}-e^{-i\theta/2}},$$

whence by (2.22),

$$C+i\,S=e^{i\alpha+\frac{n+1}{2}i\theta}\,\frac{\sin n\theta/2}{\sin \theta/2}.$$

Finally, on separating real and imaginary parts we find that

$$C=\cos\left(\alpha+\frac{n+1}{2}\theta\right)\frac{\sin n\theta/2}{\sin \theta/2}$$

and

$$S=\sin\left(\alpha+\frac{n+1}{2}\theta\right)\frac{\sin n\theta/2}{\sin \theta/2}.$$

Example 2. Show that, if n is a positive integer,

$$T=n\sin\theta+\frac{n(n-1)}{2!}\sin 2\theta+\frac{n(n-1)(n-2)}{3!}\sin 3\theta$$
$$+\ldots+\sin n\theta=(2\cos\tfrac12\theta)^n\sin\tfrac12 n\theta.$$

Proof: $(1+e^{i\theta})^n=1+ne^{i\theta}+\frac{n(n-1)}{2!}e^{2i\theta}+\ldots+e^{in\theta}$, so

that

$$T=\mathscr{I}\{(1+e^{i\theta})^n\}=\mathscr{I}\{e^{\frac12 in\theta}(e^{\frac12 i\theta}+e^{-\frac12 i\theta})^n\}$$
$$=\mathscr{I}(e^{\frac12 in\theta}\,2^n\cos^n\tfrac12\theta)=\sin\tfrac12 n\theta\,(2\cos\tfrac12\theta)^n.$$

EXERCISES ON CHAPTER TWO

1. The points AB are represented by the complex numbers $a=1-3i$ $b=-3+4i$ respectively. Find a point X on the positive real axis such that AXB is a right-angled triangle with the right angle at X.

2. Verify that the points $2+i$, $3+2i$, $2+3i$, $1+2i$ are the vertices of a square.

3. Find the region in the z-plane described by the inequality
$$|z-1|+|z-i|\leqslant 4.$$

4. Prove that the points z_1, z_2, z_3 are collinear, if and only if there exist real numbers λ_1, λ_2, λ_3, not all zero, such that $\lambda_1 z_1+\lambda_2 z_2+\lambda_3 z_3=0$ and $\lambda_1+\lambda_2+\lambda_3=0$.

5. Show that the equation $\epsilon z\bar z+\bar a z+a\bar z+\gamma=0$, where ϵ and γ are real and a is complex, represents a circle if $\epsilon\neq 0$ and $|a|^2>\epsilon\gamma$, and that it represents a straight line if $\epsilon=0$ and $a\neq 0$.

GEOMETRICAL REPRESENTATIONS

6. The quadrilateral z_1, z_2, z_3, z_4 can be inscribed in a circle if and only if the *cross ratio*
$\{z_1, z_3; z_2, z_4\} = (z_1 - z_2)(z_3 - z_4)/(z_1 - z_4)(z_3 - z_2)$ is real.

7. The vertices of a parallelogram $ABVU$ are represented by the complex numbers a, b, v, u respectively. The angle UAB is equal to α and $|UA| = \lambda|AB|$. Prove that $u = (1 - q)a + qb$ and $v = -qa + (1 + q)b$, where $q = \lambda e^{i\alpha}$.

8. Show that if $\lambda \neq 0$, 1, the equation $|(z - a)/(z - b)| = \lambda$ represents a circle which contains a or b in its interior according as $\lambda < 1$ or $\lambda > 1$.

9. Prove that if $\cos \theta = c$, $\cos 6\theta = 32c^6 - 48c^4 + 18c^2 - 1$ and $\sin 6\theta/\sin \theta = 32c^5 - 32c^3 + 6c$.

10. Express $\left\{1 + i \tan\dfrac{4m + 1}{4n}\pi\right\}^n$ in the form $a + ib$, where a and b are real, when n and m are integers.

11. Prove that
$$\frac{1 + \sin \theta + i \cos \theta}{1 + \sin \theta - i \cos \theta} = \sin \theta + i \cos \theta$$
and deduce that
$$\left(1 + \sin\frac{\pi}{5} + i \cos\frac{\pi}{5}\right)^5 + i\left(1 + \sin\frac{\pi}{5} - i \cos\frac{\pi}{5}\right)^5 = 0.$$

CHAPTER THREE

Roots of Unity

A complex number of unit modulus ($r=1$) is of the form $\exp i\theta$ or $\cos\theta + i\sin\theta$, where θ is real. In the z-plane these

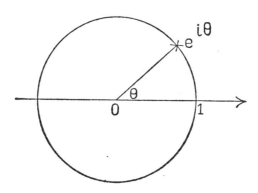

Figure 11

points are represented by the points on the circumference of the *unit circle* $x^2 + y^2 = 1$. Note that the condition $z\bar{z} = 1$ is equivalent to $\bar{z} = z^{-1}$, so that complex numbers of unit modulus are characterized by the fact that the conjugate complex coincides with the reciprocal.

We now turn to the study of a particular kind of complex numbers of unit modulus. Consider the equation

$$z^n = 1, \tag{3.1}$$

where n is a positive integer. A solution of this equation is called an nth *root of unity*. Evidently, $z = 1$ is a solution, whatever the value of n, and this is clearly the only real positive solution. When n is even, $z = -1$ also satisfies the equation, but no real number other than ± 1 can possibly occur amongst the roots of unity for any n. However, the situation is quite different, when we admit complex numbers as solutions. Suppose now that the complex number z is a solution of (3.1). Then by taking moduli in (3.1), we find that $z^n = |z|^n = 1$. Thus $|z|$ is a positive solution of (3.1) and hence $|z| = 1$. Therefore, a root of unity is necessarily a number of unit modulus, and we may put $z = \exp i\theta$. Our equation now becomes

$$\exp in\theta = \cos n\theta + i \sin n\theta = 1.$$

Comparing real parts we obtain that $\cos n\theta = 1$ and so $n\theta = 2\pi k$, where k is an integer. In other words, if z is a solution of (3.1), it must be of the form $\exp(2\pi i k/n)$. On the other hand, every number of this form is in fact a solution, for

$$\{\exp(2\pi i k/n)\}^n = \exp(2\pi ki) = 1 \quad (k = 0, \pm 1, \pm 2, \ldots).$$

It would seem at first sight that we have found infinitely many solutions, one for each integer k. However, these solutions are not all distinct. Indeed, if k_1 and k_2 differ by a whole multiple of n, say $k_2 = k_1 + sn$ (s an integer), then

$$\exp(2\pi k_2 i/n) = \exp(2\pi k_1 i/n) \exp(2\pi si) = \exp(2\pi k_1 i/n),$$

in virtue of (2.19). We may therefore confine ourselves to those solutions that correspond to $k = 0, 1, 2, \ldots, n-1$ (or to any set of n integers no two of which differ by a multiple of n). These n special solutions, namely,

$$\epsilon_0 = 1, \ \epsilon_1 = \exp(2\pi i/n) = \cos\frac{2\pi}{n} + i \sin\frac{2\pi}{n},$$

$$\epsilon_2 = \exp(4\pi i/n) = \cos\frac{4\pi}{n} + i \sin\frac{4\pi}{n}.$$

$$\epsilon_3 = \exp(6\pi i/n) = \cos\frac{6\pi}{n} + i \sin\frac{6\pi}{n}.$$

$$\cdot \quad \cdot \quad \cdot \quad \cdot \quad \cdot \quad \cdot$$

$$\epsilon_k = \exp(2k\pi i/n) = \cos\frac{2k\pi}{n} + i \sin\frac{2k\pi}{n}.$$

$$\cdot \quad \cdot \quad \cdot \quad \cdot \quad \cdot \quad \cdot$$

$$\epsilon_{n-1}=\exp(2(n-1)\pi i/n)=\cos\frac{2(n-1)\pi}{n}+i\sin\frac{2(n-1)\pi}{n}.$$

are in fact distinct. For any equality between them, say $\epsilon_k=\epsilon_l$ $(k>l)$ would lead to the equation $\exp\dfrac{2\pi i(k-l)}{n}=1$ and on comparing real parts we should find that $\cos\dfrac{2\pi(k-l)}{n}$ $=1$. Moreover, every solution of (3.1) is included in this list. For we have seen that any solution is of the form $\exp(2\pi ik/n)$ where k is an integer which may clearly be taken to lie in the range $0\leqslant k\leqslant n-1$. Notice that if ϵ is an nth root of 1, so are all its powers

$$1,\ \epsilon,\ \epsilon^2,\ \ldots,\ \epsilon^{n-1}. \qquad (3.3)$$

However, in general, these numbers are not distinct. An nth root of unity for which the powers (3.3) are distinct, is called a *primitive n^{th} root of unity*. It follows that if ϵ is a primitive n^{th} root of unity, the powers (3.3) constitute a complete set of solutions. Whatever the value of n, the number

$$\epsilon=\epsilon_1=\exp(2\pi i/n) \qquad (3.4)$$

is a primitive n^{th} root of unity, because its successive powers are identical with the solutions listed in (3.2). In fact, $\epsilon_k=\exp(2k\pi i/n)=(\exp(2\pi i/n))^k=\epsilon^k (k=0, 1, \ldots, n-1)$. When the nth roots of unity are plotted in the complex plane, they form the vertices of a regular n-gon inscribed in the unit circle, one vertex being at the point 1 on the real axis. The case $n=6$ is illustrated in Fig. 12.

Example 1. The fourth roots of unity are 1, i, -1, $-i$.

Example 2. The fifth roots of unity are

$$\epsilon_0=1,\ \epsilon_1=\cos\frac{2\pi}{5}+i\sin\frac{2\pi}{5}=\cdot3090+\cdot9511\,i,$$

$$\epsilon_2=\cos\frac{4\pi}{5}+i\sin\frac{4\pi}{5}=-\cdot8090+\cdot5878\,i.$$

$$\epsilon_3 = \cos \frac{6\pi}{5} + i \sin \frac{6\pi}{5} = -\,{\cdot}8090 - {\cdot}5878\,i.$$

$$\epsilon_4 = \cos \frac{8\pi}{5} + i \sin \frac{8\pi}{5} = {\cdot}3090 - {\cdot}9511\,i.$$

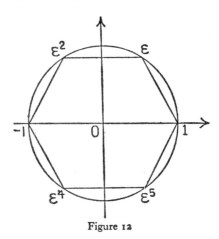

Figure 12

Example 3. If ϵ is a primitive n^{th} root of unity,
$$1 + \epsilon^s + \epsilon^{2s} + \ldots + \epsilon^{(n-1)s}$$
is equal to 0 if s is not a multiple of n and is equal to n if s is a multiple of n.

For if $s = nq$, $\epsilon^s = 1$ and each of the n terms of the sum is equal to unity. On the other hand, if $s \neq nq$, we can write $s = nq + r$, where $0 < r < 1$. Then $\epsilon^s = \epsilon^r \neq 1$, and the sum may be treated as a geometric progression with ratio ϵ^s. Thus it is equal to $(\epsilon^{ns} - 1)/(\epsilon^s - 1) = 0$.

The *cube roots of unity* are of especial interest in certain electrical problems. They are the roots of the equation

$$z^3 - 1 = 0. \tag{3.5}$$

Of course, this equation can be solved from first principles, and there is no need to invoke the general theory. Indeed, since $z^3 - 1 = (z - 1)(z^2 + z + 1)$, the equation (3.5) is satis-

36

fied either if $z=1$ or if $z^2+z+1=0$ and so $z=\frac{1}{2}(-1\pm i\sqrt3)$.
In the traditional notation, the three cube roots of unity are

$$1,\ \omega=-\tfrac{1}{2}+i\,\tfrac{1}{2}\sqrt3,\ \overline{\omega}=-\tfrac{1}{2}-i\,\tfrac{1}{2}\sqrt3. \qquad (3.6)$$

This agrees with the general theory, according to which the two complex cube roots of unity are

$$(\epsilon=)\omega=\cos\frac{2\pi}{3}+i\sin\frac{2\pi}{3},\ \omega^2=\cos\frac{4\pi}{3}+i\sin\frac{4\pi}{3}.$$

We observe that $\overline{\omega}=\omega^2$, a fact that can easily be proved directly. For, since $|\omega|=1$, we have that $\overline{\omega}=1/\omega=\omega^3/\omega=\omega^2$. Finally, we record the relation

$$\omega^2+\omega+1=0, \qquad (3.7)$$

obtained when we established (3.6).

Example 1. Prove the identity
$$x^3+y^3+z^3-3xyz=(x+y+z)(x+\omega y+\omega^2 z)(x+\omega^2 y+\omega z),$$
where x, y and z are indeterminates.

The reader will have no difficulty in verifying the result by multiplying out the brackets on the right, preferably starting with the last two brackets. A neater way, which uses simple properties of determinants is as follows: let

$$\Delta=\begin{vmatrix} x & z & y \\ y & x & z \\ z & y & x \end{vmatrix}$$

By expanding the determinant in the usual way we find that $\Delta=x^3+y^3+z^3-3xyz$. On the other hand, by adding the second and the third rows to the first row, we see that $x+y+z$ is a factor of Δ. Next we modify the first row by adding to it ω times the second and ω^2 times the third row. The first row now reads

$$x+\omega y+\omega^2 z,\ z+\omega x+\omega^2 y,\ y+\omega z+\omega^2 x$$

that is

$$x+wy+w^2z,\ w(x+wy+w^2z),\ w^2(x+wy+w^2z).$$

This makes it plain that $x+\omega y+\omega^2 z$ is a factor of Δ.

Similarly on replacing ω by $\omega^2(=\overline{\omega})$ we find that $x+\omega^2 y+\omega z$ is a factor of Δ. Since Δ is of degree 3 in each indeterminate, there can be no further factors except a constant. By examining the coefficient of x^3 we find that the constant factor is in fact unity. This establishes the result.

Example 2. The complex numbers ϵ_1, ϵ_2, ϵ_3 are of unit modulus and satisfy $\epsilon_1 + \epsilon_2 + \epsilon_3 = 0$. Prove that

$$\left(\frac{\epsilon_2}{\epsilon_1}\right)^3 = \left(\frac{\epsilon_3}{\epsilon_2}\right)^3 = \left(\frac{\epsilon_1}{\epsilon_3}\right)^3 = 1.$$

When interpreted geometrically, the conditions are equivalent to the statement that the vectors ϵ_1, ϵ_2, ϵ_3 form the sides of an equilateral triangle. Therefore $\arg(\epsilon_2/\epsilon_1) = \pm 2\pi/3$, the sign depending on the orientation of the triangle. Hence $\epsilon_2 = \omega\epsilon_1$ or $\epsilon_2 = \bar{\omega}\epsilon_1$, and in both cases $(\epsilon_2/\epsilon_1)^3 = 1$. The other relations are proved by similar arguments.

Having now learned how to extract the nth root of unity, we shall have no difficulty in finding the n determinations of $a^{1/n}$, where a is any given complex number. (We may clearly assume that $a \neq 0$.) Let $a = p \exp i\alpha$ be the polar form of a and assume that $z = r \exp i\theta$ is a solution of the equation

$$z^n = a. \tag{3.8}$$

Then $r^n \exp(i\theta n) = p \exp i\alpha$, whence $r = \sqrt[n]{p}$, by which we mean the unique positive value of the root and $\theta n = \alpha + 2\pi k$ ($k = 0, \pm 1, \pm 2, \ldots$), so that $\theta = (\alpha + 2\pi k)/n$. We may therefore assert that $a^{1/n} = \sqrt[n]{p} \exp((\alpha + 2\pi k)i/n)$, because the nth power of the number on the right is equal to $p \exp i\alpha = a$, whatever the value of the integer k. Confining attention to distinct determinations of $a^{1/n}$, we may write

$$a^{1/n} = \sqrt[n]{p} \exp\left(\frac{i\alpha}{n}\right)\epsilon_k \quad (k = 0, 1, 2, \ldots, n-1), \tag{3.9}$$

where $\epsilon_k = \exp\left(\frac{2\pi k i}{n}\right)$ runs through all the nth roots of unity.

Note the following rule: if b is a particular root of (3.8), the complete set of roots can be expressed in the form $b, b\epsilon, b\epsilon^2, \ldots, b\epsilon^{n-1}$, where ϵ is a primitive n^{th} root of unity. If $a = p \exp i\alpha$, we may put $b = \sqrt[n]{p} \exp(i\alpha/n)$.

Example 3. Evaluate $(2-2i)^{1/4}$. In this case $p=|a|=\sqrt{8}$ and $\alpha=\arg a=-\pi/4$. Hence we may take $b=$ $\sqrt[8]{8}\left(\cos\dfrac{\pi}{16}-i\sin\dfrac{\pi}{16}\right)$. The four values of $(2-2i)^{1/4}$ are therefore b, bi, $-b$ and $-bi$.

Example 4. Obtain the three cube roots of $8i$. Here we have $a=8i=8\exp(i\pi/2)$, $|a|=8$, $\beta=\pi/2$. Hence we may put $b=2\exp(i\pi/6)=2(\cos(\pi/6)+i\sin(\pi/6))=\sqrt{3}+i$. The other two roots are $b\omega=2\exp\left(\dfrac{i\pi}{6}+\dfrac{2i\pi}{3}\right)=2\exp\left(\dfrac{5i\pi}{6}\right)$ $=-\sqrt{3}+i$ and $b\omega^2=2\exp\left(\dfrac{i\pi}{6}+\dfrac{4i\pi}{3}\right)=2\exp\left(\dfrac{3i\pi}{2}\right)=-2i$.

In the elementary theory of algebraic equation it is shown that if the roots of the polynomial equation
$$f(z)=a_0z^n+a_1z^{n-1}+a_2z^{n-2}+\ldots+a_{n-1}z+a_n=0$$
are $\alpha_1, \alpha_2, \ldots, \alpha_n$, then the polynomial can be resolved into n linear factors, thus
$$f(z)=a_0(z-\alpha_1)(z-\alpha_2)(z-\alpha_3)\ldots(z-\alpha_n).$$
The validity of this result is not affected if we admit complex numbers for the coefficients and for the roots of the equation.

Applying these remarks to the polynomial z^n-1, we obtain the identity
$$z^n-1=(z-1)(z-\epsilon)(z-\epsilon^2)\ldots(z-\epsilon^{n-1}), \quad (3.10)$$
where ϵ is a primitive n^{th} root of unity (see (3.4)). Combining (3.10) with the well-known formula
$$z^n-1=(z-1)(z^{n-1}+z^{n-2}+\ldots+z+1)$$
we deduce that
$$z^{n-1}+z^{n-2}+\ldots+z+1=(z-\epsilon)(z-\epsilon^2)\ldots(z-\epsilon^{n-1}).$$
$$(3.11)$$

Example 5. Show that, if ϵ is a primitive n^{th} root of unity,
$$(1-\epsilon)(1-\epsilon^2)\ldots(1-\epsilon^{n-1})=n.$$

This follows at once by putting $z=1$ in (3.11).

The factors on the right of (3.10) are linear, that is of the first degree in z, but they involve the number ϵ, which is complex when $n>2$. If we admit quadratic factors, the splitting can be accomplished with real factors only. This is based on the observation that if γ is any complex number,

$$(z-\gamma)(z-\bar{\gamma})=z^2-(\gamma+\bar{\gamma})z+\gamma\bar{\gamma}$$

is a quadratic with real coefficients, since both $\gamma+\bar{\gamma}(=2\mathscr{R}\gamma)$ and $\gamma\bar{\gamma}(=|\gamma|^2)$ are real. Now we know (p. 11) that the complex roots of the equation (3.1) occur in conjugate complex pairs. A typical root can be written ϵ^r, and $\overline{\epsilon^r}=(\bar{\epsilon})^r=(\epsilon^{-1})^r$ $=1\epsilon^{-r}=\epsilon^n\epsilon^{-r}=\epsilon^{n-r}$. Thus the pairs of conjugate complex roots are as follows

$$\epsilon,\ \epsilon^{n-1};\ \epsilon^2,\ \epsilon^{n-2};\ \ldots;\ \epsilon^s,\ \epsilon^{n-s}, \tag{3.12}$$

where $s=\frac{1}{2}(n-1)$, when n is odd and $s=\frac{1}{2}(n-2)$, when n is even. Notice that when n is even, $\epsilon^{\frac{1}{2}n}=-1$ is a 'self-conjugate', that is a real n^{th} root of unity. Let us now take the special primitive root (3.4). Then

$$(z-\epsilon^r)(z-\epsilon^{n-r})=(z-\epsilon^r)(z-\epsilon^{-r})=z^2-(\epsilon^r+\epsilon^{-r})z+1$$
$$=z^2-2\cos\frac{2\pi r}{n}z+1$$

in virtue of (2.22). Thus the final factorization is

$$\left.\begin{array}{l} z^n-1=(z-1)\displaystyle\prod_{r=1}^{\frac{1}{2}(n-1)}\left(z^2-2\cos\frac{2\pi r}{n}z+1\right),\ \text{when }n\text{ is odd} \\[1em] z^n-1=(z-1)(z+1)\displaystyle\prod_{r=1}^{\frac{1}{2}(n-2)}\left(z^2-2\cos\frac{2\pi r}{n}z+1\right),\ \text{when }n\text{ is} \\ \hspace{10cm}\text{even} \end{array}\right\} \tag{3.13}$$

A similar procedure leads to the factorization of z^n-a, where a is a given complex number. In fact,

$$z^n-a=(z-b)(z-\epsilon b)(z-\epsilon^2 b)\ldots(z-\epsilon^{n-1}b),$$

where b is any number such that $b^n=a$.

ROOTS OF UNITY

The algebraical identities which we have just established, can be used to derive numerous trigonometrical relations.

Example 6. Show that

$$z^6+z^3+1= \left(z^2- 2z \cos\frac{2\pi}{9}+1\right)\left(z^2- 2z \cos\frac{4\pi}{9}+1\right)$$
$$\left(z^2- 2z \cos\frac{8\pi}{9}+1\right) \quad (3.14)$$

and deduce that

$$2 \cos 3\theta+1=8 \left(\cos \theta- \cos\frac{2\pi}{9}\right)\left(\cos \theta- \cos\frac{4\pi}{9}\right)$$
$$\left(\cos \theta- \cos\frac{8\pi}{9}\right) \quad (3.15)$$

Use (3.13) when $n=9$ and observe that the factor that corresponds to $r=3$, is $z^2- 2z \cos\frac{2\pi}{3}+1=z^2+z+1$, the remaining three quadratic factors being as on the right-hand side of (3.14). This expression is therefore equal to $(z^9- 1)/(z- 1)$ $(z^2+z+1) = (z^9- 1)/(z^3- 1) = z^6+z^3+1$, which proves (3.14). Next, divide (3.14) throughout by z^3 and then put $z=e^i$. With this value of z, $z+z^{-1}=2 \cos \theta$, $z^3+z^{-3}=2 \cos 3\theta$, and (3.15) is an immediate consequence.

EXERCISES ON CHAPTER THREE

1. Write down all the sixth roots of unity in the form $a+ib$ (a, b real).

2. Evaluate $i^{1/4}$.

3. Evaluate $(2+2i)^{1/3}$.

4. Show that if $|z|=1$ and $\mathscr{R}z= -\frac{1}{2}$, then $z^3=1$.

5. Prove that, if $\omega= -\frac{1}{2}+\frac{1}{2}i\sqrt{3}$, (i) $a^3+b^3=(a+b)(a\omega+b\omega^2)(a\omega^2+b\omega)$,
(ii)$(a+b+c)^3+(a+b\omega+c\omega^2)^3+(a+b\omega^2+c\omega)^3=3(a^3+b^3+c^3+6abc)$.

6. Show that the complex numbers o, u, v correspond to the vertices of an equilateral triangle if and only if $u^2+v^2=uv$.

7. Deduce from Ex. 6 that the numbers z_1, z_2, z_3 correspond to the vertices of an equilateral triangle if and only if
$$z_1^2+z_2^2+z_3^2=z_2z_3+z_3z_1+z_1z_2.$$

41

ROOTS OF UNITY

8. Write down the roots of $z^3 + 1 = 0$ and plot them in the z-plane. Resolve $z^3 + 1$ into real quadratic factors and deduce that
$$\cos 4\theta = 8 \ \left(\cos\theta - \cos\frac{\pi}{8}\right)\left(\cos\theta - \cos\frac{3\pi}{8}\right)\left(\cos\theta - \cos\frac{5\pi}{8}\right)$$
$$\left(\cos\theta - \cos\frac{7\pi}{8}\right).$$

9. Resolve $z^5 + 1$ into linear and quadratic factors with real coefficients Deduce that $4 \sin\frac{\pi}{10} \cos\frac{\pi}{5} = 1$.

10. Show that the roots of $(z-1)^6 + (z+1)^6 = 0$ are
$$\pm i \cot\frac{\pi}{12}, \ \pm i \cot\frac{5\pi}{12}, \ \pm i.$$

CHAPTER FOUR

Elementary Functions of a Complex Variable

---

1. INTRODUCTION

In the preceding chapters we studied complex numbers from an algebraical point of view, coupled with geometrical interpretations, and this enabled us to arrive at a sensible and consistent definition of powers z^r, where r is an integer. We also discussed fractional powers and their many-valuedness. Thus we are in the position to handle expressions like $(z^{\frac{1}{2}}+2z^{-5})/(3z^2+i)$, in which several such powers are combined.

However, there remains a vast class of functions, familiar to the reader from the real field, which has not yet been extended to the case of a complex variable. We have already mentioned, without proof, the properties of $\exp z$, when z is complex, but we have not considered the other 'elementary' functions $\sin z$, $\cos z$, and $\log z$.

It is clear that the geometrical definition of $\sin \theta$ as (opposite side)/(hypotenuse) in a right-angled triangle loses its meaning, when the 'angle' θ is replaced by an arbitrary complex number. We therefore abandon the geometrical approach and base our definitions on the series

$$\exp z = 1 + \frac{z}{1!} + \frac{z^2}{2!} + \frac{z^3}{3!} + \cdots \qquad (4.1)$$

$$\sin z = z - \frac{z^3}{3!} + \frac{z^5}{5!} - \frac{z^7}{7!} + \cdots \qquad (4.2)$$

$$\cos z = 1 - \frac{z^2}{2!} + \frac{z^4}{4!} - \frac{z^6}{6!} + \cdots \qquad (4.3)$$

To be sure, this raises the question as to what is meant by

an infinite series with complex terms, and we are obliged at this stage to embark upon a digression on the convergence of complex sequences and series. Although we shall endeavour to make the next two sections as nearly self-contained as possible, the reader is expected to be acquainted with the corresponding† work on real sequences and series.

2. SEQUENCES

The notion of convergence of a sequence of complex numbers can be reduced to the idea of a null-sequence of real numbers, that is of a sequence of real numbers, which tend to zero.

Definition. *The sequence of complex numbers*
$$z_1, \ z_2, \ z_3, \ \ldots, \ z_n, \ \ldots$$
is said to converge to c, in symbols, $z_n \to c$, as $n \to \infty$, if and only if $|z_n - c| \to 0$.

The geometrical significance of this definition is easily

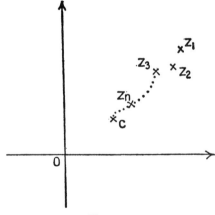

Figure 13

explained: plot the numbers z_1, z_2, z_3, ... in the z-plane and consider the sequence of distances of these points from their presumed limit, thus

$$|z_1 - c|, |z_2 - c|, \ldots, |z_n - c|, \ldots \qquad (4.4)$$

This is a sequence of non-negative (real) numbers, and the assertion that $z_n \to c$ means that the points z_1, z_2, ... cluster around c in the sense that their distances from c tend to zero as n tends to infinity.

An alternative approach is to split the complex numbers into their real and imaginary parts, say $z_n = x_n + iy_n$, whence the problem of convergence is reduced to the consideration of the two real sequences $\{x_n\}$ and $\{y_n\}$. The equivalence of the two methods is contained in the following theorem.

Theorem. *The sequence $z_n = x_n + iy_n$ tends to $c = a + ib$, if and only if simultaneously $x_n \to a$ and $y_n \to b$.*

Proof. (i) Suppose that $z_n \to c$ in accordance with our definition (p. 44). Thus $|z_n - c| \to 0$ and hence $|z_n - c|^2 \to 0$, or more explicitly,

$$p_n = (x_n - a)^2 + (y_n - b)^2 \to 0.$$

Recalling now the definition of convergence for real sequences (note that x_n, y_n and p_n are real), we may infer, roughly speaking, that p_n becomes arbitrarily small as n increases. But $(x_n - a)^2$ and $(y_n - b)^2$ are each smaller than p_n, or at least not greater, whence it follows that $(x_n - a)^2 \to 0$ and $(y_n - b)^2 \to 0$, and therefore

$$x_n \to a, \ y_n \to b. \qquad (4.5)$$

It is not difficult to recast this argument into a rigorous form but we refrain from doing so, as it would hardly be helpful to the reader.

(ii) Conversely, assume that $x_n \to a$ and $y_n \to b$. Then retracing the steps in the preceding paragraph, we deduce that $(x_n - a)^2 \to 0$ and $(y_n - b)^2 \to 0$ and hence that $(x_n - a)^2 +$

$(y_n - b)^2 \to 0$. This means that $|z_n - c|^2 \to 0$, and finally $|z_n - c| \to 0$. Thus $z_n \to c$ according to the original definition.

Corollary. If $z_n \to c$, then $|z_n| \to |c|$.

For $\left| |z_n| - |c| \right| \leqslant |z_n - c|$ by (2.4) so that $z_n \to c$ implies that $|z_n| \to |c|$.

Notice that $\lim z_n$ cannot possibly exist, if $|z_n|$ fails to tend to a finite limit.

Examples.

(i) $z_n = \dfrac{(3 + in)^2}{n^2}$. Separating into real and imaginary parts we have that $z_n = \dfrac{9 - n^2}{n^2} + \dfrac{6i}{n} = x_n + iy_n$, where $x_n = \dfrac{9 - n^2}{n^2}$ $= -1 + \dfrac{9}{n^2} \to -1$ and $y_n = \dfrac{6}{n} \to 0$. Hence $z_n \to -1 + 0i = -1$.

(ii) $z_n = \left(\dfrac{2}{3} + \dfrac{3i}{4}\right)^n$. Since $\left|\dfrac{2}{3} + \dfrac{3i}{4}\right|^2 = \dfrac{4}{9} + \dfrac{9}{16} = \dfrac{145}{144} > 1$, it follows that $|z_n| = (145/144)^{\frac{1}{2}n}$ tends to infinity, and hence $\lim z_n$ does not exist.

(iii) $z_n = (-1)^n + \dfrac{i}{n}$. Here z_n does not tend to a limit, because the real parts, that is $x_n = (-1)^n$, do not form a convergent real sequence.

(iv) *If* $|z| < 1$, *then* $z^n \to 0$, *as* $n \to 0$. For we know that the real sequence† $|z|^n$ tends to zero. Since $|z|^n = |z^n|$, $|z^n| \to 0$ or $|z^n - 0| \to 0$ which means that $z_n \to 0$.

(v) $z_n = \left(\cos\dfrac{\pi}{n} + i\sin\dfrac{\pi}{n}\right)^{2n+1}$. By de Moivre's theorem $z_n = \cos\dfrac{(2n+1)\pi}{n} + i\sin\dfrac{(2n+1)\pi}{n}$. Since $\dfrac{2n+1}{n} \to 2$, it follows from the continuity of the functions $\cos\theta$ and $\sin\theta$ that $\lim z_n = \cos 2\pi + i\sin 2\pi = 1$.

† J. A. Green, *loc. cit.*, Example **2**, p. 6.

The rules for calculating with convergent sequences of complex numbers are analogous to those for sequences of real numbers.†

Rules. *If $z_n \to c$ and $w_n \to d$, then*
   (i) $z_n + w_n \to c + d$,   (ii) $z_n - w_n \to c - d$,   (iii) $z_n w_n \to cd$,
(iv) $z_n/w_n \to c/d$, *where in* (iv) $w_n \neq 0$ *for all* n *and* $d \neq 0$.

We can either prove these results from first principles by arguments similar to those used in the real case, or else we resolve each complex number into its real and imaginary part and then apply the known rules for real sequences. Thus let $z_n = x_n + iy_n$, $w_n = u_n + iv_n$, $c = a + ib$, $d = e + if$. Then, for example, $z_n w_n = (x_n u_n - y_n v_n) + i(y_n u_n + x_n v_n)$. Now our hypotheses imply that $x_n \to a$, $u_n \to e$, $y_n \to b$, $v_n \to f$. Hence $z_n w_n \to (ae - bf) + i(be + af) = (a + ib)(e + if) = cd$.

3. SERIES

The definition of convergence of an infinite series
$$w_1 + w_2 + \ldots + w_n + \ldots \tag{4.6}$$
with complex terms $w_n = x_n + iy_n$ is the same as for series with real terms.‡ In both cases the concept of convergence of a series is reduced to the more fundamental notion of convergence of a sequence.

Definition. *The series*
$$w_1 + w_2 + \ldots + w_n + \ldots \tag{4.6}$$
is said to converge to the sum W, *if the sequence of partial sums* $W_1, W_2, \ldots, W_n, \ldots$ *defined by*
   $W_1 = w_1$, $W_2 = w_1 + w_2$, ..., $W_n = w_1 + w_2 + \ldots + w_n$, ...
converges to W *in the sense of the definition of section 2. The series is said to diverge if the sequence of partial sums diverges.*

† J. A. Green, *loc. cit.*, Chapter I, section 6.
‡ See J. A. Green, *loc. cit.*, p. 28.

On applying the Theorem of p. 45 to the sequence of partial sums we arrive at an alternative definition which states that the convergence of (4.6) is equivalent to the simultaneous convergence of the real series

$$u_1 + u_2 + \ldots + u_n + \ldots \tag{4.7}$$

and

$$v_1 + v_2 + \ldots + v_n + \ldots \tag{4.8}$$

formed by the real and imaginary parts respectively. For if we denote the nth partial sums of these series by U_n and V_n respectively, we have that $W_n = U_n + iV_n$, and we know that the complex limit formula $\lim W_n = W = U + iV$, is equivalent to the pair of real formulae $\lim U_n = U$, $\lim V_n = V$.

Thus it follows that (4.6) diverges if either (4.7) or (4.8) diverges. For example, the series $\sum \frac{n+i}{n^2}$ diverges because the series of real parts, that is, $\Sigma(1/n)$ diverges.

Another useful test of divergence is furnished by the fact that *ΣW_n certainly diverges if the sequence $\{W_n\}$ does not tend to zero*. For in that case either $\{U_n\}$ or $\{V_n\}$ does not tend to zero, so that either (4.7) or (4.8) diverges.

The splitting of a complex series into real and imaginary parts is often laborious and, as we have seen, involves testing two real series for convergence. For most practical purposes it is sufficient to establish *absolute* convergence, which is defined as in the real case.†

Definition. *The series $w_1 + w_2 + \ldots$ is said to converge absolutely, if the series*

$$|w_1| + |w_2| + \ldots + |w_n| + \ldots \tag{4.9}$$

converges.

The terms of (4.9) are, of course, real and non-negative, and this series can be investigated by means of the familiar tests. The importance of the concept of absolute convergence stems from the following fact.

A.   † J. Green, *loc. cit.*, p. 45.

Theorem. *An absolutely convergent series is convergent.*

Proof. Assume then that (4.9) converges. Since $|w_n| = (u_n^2 + v_n^2)^{\frac{1}{2}} \geqslant (u_n^2)^{\frac{1}{2}} = |u_n|$ and since similarly
$$|w_n| \geqslant |v_n|,$$
the comparison test for real series with non-negative terms†
shows that the series (4.7) and (4.8) are absolutely convergent and hence convergent.

Examples.

(i) $\sum \dfrac{(-1)^n + i \cos n\theta}{n^2} = \sum \dfrac{(-1)^n}{n^2} + i \sum \dfrac{\cos n\theta}{n^2}$ converges,
because the real and the imaginary parts each form a convergent series. In fact, the series converges absolutely, since
$$\left| \frac{(-1)^n + i \cos n\theta}{n^2} \right| \leqslant \frac{1 + |\cos n\theta|}{n^2} \leqslant \frac{2}{n^2}. \left[\text{This step uses (2.1)} \right.$$

(ii) $\sum \left(\dfrac{2+3i}{3-2i} \right)^n$ diverges, because the general term does not tend to zero, for
$$\left| \left(\frac{2+3i}{3-2i} \right)^n \right| = \left| \frac{2+3i}{3-2i} \right|^n = \left(\frac{4+9}{9+4} \right)^{n/2} = 1$$
for all n (see p. 48).

(iii) $\sum \left(\dfrac{z}{1-z} \right)^n$ converges absolutely provided that $|z/(1-z)| < 1$. This condition means that z is closer to 0 than to 1, that is, $\mathscr{R}z < \frac{1}{2}$. (Alternatively, we can obtain this result by calculation, thus $|z|^2 < |1-z|^2$ means that $x^2 + y^2 < (1-x)^2 + y^2$ and so $x < \frac{1}{2}$.)

4. POWER SERIES

A power series is a series of the form
$$c_0 + c_1 z + c_2 z^2 + c_3 z^3 + \ldots + c_n z^n + \ldots, \tag{4.10}$$
where $z = x + iy$ is a complex variable and where the coefficients $c_0, c_1, c_2, \ldots$ are given numbers, in general com-

† J. A. Green, *loc. cit.*, p. 34

plex. It may happen that the series converges for all z, obviously a very desirable situation, or again, at the other extreme, for no value of z except zero, evidently a rather useless case. In general, there exists a positive number R such that (4.10) converges absolutely if $|z| < R$ and diverges if $|z| > R$. We omit the proof of this fact, but we note its geometrical interpretation, namely that each point of the

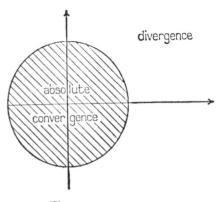

Figure 14

open circle $|z| < R$ (that is, exclusive of the boundary) is a point of absolute convergence whilst each point outside the circle is a point of divergence. This leaves out of account the points on the circumference of the circle. Their classification is often a difficult task and will not concern us here. The number R is called the *radius of convergence*, and it is a useful convention to put $R = \infty$ when the series converges (absolutely) in the whole plane.

The determination of the radius of convergence is an important problem. Notice that it involves only the series

$$|c_0| + |c_1 z| + |c_2 z^2| + \dots \qquad (4.11)$$

with real non-negative terms. In many cases R can be found by an application of the ratio test to (4.11). (It will hardly be necessary to warn the reader that the ratio test must never be used for the power series itself or any other series whose terms are not positive.)

Examples.

(i) $1+z+z^2+\ldots+z^n+\ldots$. In order to examine for absolute convergence we consider the limit, as $n\to\infty$, of the ratio $|z^n|/|z^{n-1}|=|z|$. Since the ratio happens to be independent of n, it follows that $\lim |z^n|/|z^{n-1}|=|z|$. The ratio test now tells us that the series converges absolutely when $|z|<1$ and that it diverges when $|z|>1$. Thus in this case $R=1$. In fact, when $|z|<1$, it is shown as in the real case, that $1+z+z^2+\ldots+z^n+\ldots=(1-z)^{-1}$.

(ii) The series

$$E(z)=1+\frac{z}{1!}+\frac{z^2}{2!}+\frac{z^3}{3!}+\ldots+\frac{z^n}{n!}+\ldots \qquad (4.12)$$

converges absolutely for all z. The proof is the same as in the real case.† Indeed, $\lim\left|\frac{z^{n+1}}{(n+1)!}\right|\Big/\left|\frac{z^n}{n!}\right|=\lim\frac{|z|}{n+1}=0;$ irrespective of the value of z.

(iii) The series $C(z)=1-\frac{z^2}{2!}+\frac{z^4}{4!}-z\frac{6}{6!}+\ldots$ and

$S(z)=z-\frac{z^3}{3!}+\frac{z^5}{5!}-\frac{z^7}{7!}+\ldots$ also converge for all z, as the reader can readily prove.

As long as the variable is restricted to lie inside the circle of convergence, the manipulation of power series is in many ways analogous to that of finite sums (polynomials). Thus two power series may be added and subtracted in the obvious way and if

$$f(z)=a_0+a_1z+a_2z^2+\ldots$$

and

$$g(w)=b_0+b_1w+b_2w^2+\ldots$$

both converge absolutely for certain values of z and w, $f(z)g(w)=a_0b_0+(a_1b_0z+a_0b_1w)+(a_2b_0z^2+a_1b_1zw+a_0b_2w^2)\ldots$

† J. A. Green, *loc. cit.*, p. 48

Thus absolutely convergent power series may be multiplied term by term, and the terms may be arranged in any manner,[†] for example according to increasing degrees in the variables z and w.

Example.

$$(1-z)^{-2}=(1-z)^{-1}(1-z)^{-1}$$
$$=(1+z+z^2+\ldots)(1+z+z^2+\ldots)$$
$$=1+2z+3z^2+4z^3+\ldots$$

Complex series are sometimes a useful tool for obtaining results about real series. The following example will serve as an illustration. In the formula $(1-z)^{-1}=1+z+z^2+\ldots$ ($|z|<1$) put $z=r\,e^{i\theta}$ ($r<1$) and compare real parts. Thus

$$1+r\cos\theta+r^2\cos 2\theta+\ldots=\mathscr{R}(1-re^{i\theta})^{-1}$$
$$=\frac{1-r\cos\theta}{1-2r\cos\theta+r^2}.$$

Assume now that $0<\theta<\tfrac{1}{2}\pi$. It follows that $0<\cos\theta<1$, so that the last equation is valid for $r=\cos\theta$. Hence

$$1+(\cos\theta)^2+(\cos\theta)^2\cos 2\theta+(\cos\theta)^3\cos 3\theta+\ldots$$
$$=\frac{1-\cos^2\theta}{1-\cos^2\theta}=1$$

and therefore

$$\cos\theta+\cos\theta\cos 2\theta+(\cos\theta)^2\cos 3\theta$$
$$+(\cos\theta)^3\cos 4\theta+\ldots=0.$$

5. THE FUNCTIONS e^z, $\cos z$, $\sin z$

We have seen that the infinite series $E(z)$, $C(z)$ and $S(z)$ which we discussed in the preceding section, converge for every value of z. In other words, they are functions of z, defined for all values of z. When $z=x$, where x is real, these series agree with the expansions[‡] of the familiar functions exp x (or e^x), sin x and cos x, which shows that our definitions are reasonable. Henceforth we shall write

[†] See J. A. Green, *loc. cit.*, pp. 51-4.
[‡] P. J. Hilton, *Differential Calculus*, p. 27 and p. 44.

$\exp z$, (or e^z), $\cos z$ and $\sin z$ in place of $E(z)$, $C(z)$ and $S(z)$ respectively. All relevant properties of these functions must be derived, directly or indirectly, from their definitions as power series, as will now be illustrated in a few simple cases.

(i) The most important property of the exponential function is the *functional equation*

$$\exp z \ \exp w = \exp (z+w) \qquad (4.12)$$

The proof† is exactly the same as for a real variable and need not be repeated here. In particular, on putting $w = -z$, we see that the relation $\exp z \ \exp (-z) = \exp 0 = 1$ holds also for complex z, whence it follows that the exponential function is never zero.

The reader should, however, beware of uncritically transferring unproved assertions from the real to the complex domain. For instance, the statement that $\exp x$ is always positive, is true for real values of x, but for complex z the series for $\exp z$ need no longer be real, let alone positive. For example, we know that $\exp (\pi i) = -1$.

(ii) Replacing z by iz in the definition (4.12) we find that

$$\exp (iz) = 1 + \frac{iz}{1!} - \frac{z^2}{2!} - \frac{iz^3}{3!} + \frac{z^4}{4!} + \frac{iz^5}{5!} - \frac{z^6}{6!} - \cdots$$

$$= \left(1 - \frac{z^2}{2!} + \frac{z^4}{4!} - \ \right) + i \left(z - \frac{z^3}{3!} + \frac{z^5}{5!} - \cdots \right).$$

Thus we obtain the fundamental relation

$$\exp iz = \cos z + i \sin z; \qquad (4.14)$$

a special case was already mentioned on p. 29. We recall that (4.14) leads to the important equation $\exp (2\pi i) = 1$ and hence to the fact that $\exp z$ is periodic with period $2\pi i$. Since (4.14) holds for arbitrary complex values, we may replace z by $-z$, thus

$$\exp (-iz) = \cos (-z) + i \sin (-z).$$

Now inspection of the defining series shows that $\cos z$ is an *even* function and that $\sin z$ is an *odd* function, that is

† J. A. Green, *loc. cit.*, pp. 52-3.

FUNCTIONS OF A COMPLEX VARIABLE

$$\cos(-z) = \cos z, \sin(-z) = -\sin z. \quad (4.15)$$

It follows that

$$\exp(-iz) = \cos z - i \sin z. \quad (4.16)$$

Combining (4.14) and (4.16) we obtain that

$$\left.\begin{array}{l} \cos z = \dfrac{1}{2}(e^{iz} + e^{-iz}) \\[2mm] \sin z = \dfrac{1}{2i}(e^{iz} - e^{-iz}). \end{array}\right\} \quad (4.17)$$

Thus it has become apparent that in the complex domain the functions cos z and sin z are little more than abbreviations of simple combinations of exponential functions. The number of elementary functions has therefore virtually been reduced from three to one. This fact remains hidden, if we confine ourselves to real variables. Note that (4.17) reduces to (2.22), when $z = \theta$, where θ is real. In this book, we take the familiar properties of cos θ and sin θ for granted. In particular, we do not intend to 'define' π and to prove that cos $\frac{1}{2}\pi = 0$ and sin $\frac{1}{2}\pi = 1$, etc. On the other hand, it is relevant to ask whether formulae like the *addition theorem*

$$\sin(z+w) = \sin z \cos w + \cos z \sin w \quad (4.18)$$

still hold when z and w are complex. In order to prove this result consider

$$2 \sin z \cos w = 2\frac{e^{iz} - e^{-iz}}{2i}\frac{e^{iw} + e^{-iw}}{2}$$

$$= \frac{1}{2i}\{(e^{iz} - e^{-iz})(e^{iw} + e^{-iw})\}$$

$$= \frac{1}{2i}\{e^{i(z+w)} - e^{-i(z+w)} + e^{i(z-w)} - e^{-i(z-w)}\},$$

that is

$$2 \sin z \cos w = \sin(z+w) + \sin(z-w).$$

On interchanging z and w we derive the further relation

$$2 \cos z \sin w = \sin(z+w) - \sin(z-w),$$

THE FUNCTIONS e^z, $\cos z$, $\sin z$

whence (4.18) follows at once by addition. In particular, when $w=\frac{1}{2}\pi$, we see that

$$\sin\left(\tfrac{1}{2}\pi+z\right)=\cos z, \qquad (4.19)$$

and similarly, that $\sin(\pi+z)= -\sin z$, $\cos(\pi+z)= -\cos z$, etc. The remaining addition formulae, namely,

$$\cos(z+w)=\cos z\cos w-\sin z\sin w$$
$$\sin(z-w)=\sin z\cos w-\cos z\sin w$$
$$\cos(z-w)=\cos z\cos w+\sin z\sin w$$

easily follow from (4.18) by substituting for w either $\frac{1}{2}\pi+w$ or $-w$. Note that when $z=w$, the last equation reduces to

$$\cos^2 z+\sin^2 z=1. \qquad (4.20)$$

From this relation it must not be inferred, as in the real case, that $\cos z$ and $\sin z$ have moduli less than unity. For these functions may in general take complex values, and the square is no longer the same as the square of the modulus. For example, let p be a positive number. Then

$$\cos(ip)=\tfrac{1}{2}(e^{-p}+e^{p})>\tfrac{1}{2}e^{p},$$

since $e^{-p}>0$. Thus we see that $\cos ip$ is real and can exceed any bound, if p is sufficiently great.

The remaining trigonometric functions are less important and are defined in terms of $\cos z$ and $\sin z$ in the usual way. For example,

$$\tan z=\frac{\sin z}{\cos z}=\frac{1}{i}\frac{e^{iz}-e^{-iz}}{e^{iz}+e^{-iz}}.$$

The reader will observe that our definition of $\sin z$ and $\cos z$ is analogous to the definition of the hyperbolic functions[†]

$$\cosh z=\tfrac{1}{2}(e^{z}+e^{-z}),\ \sinh z=\tfrac{1}{2}(e^{z}-e^{-z}) \qquad (4.21)$$

Comparing (4.17) and (4.21) we deduce the simple relations

$$\left.\begin{array}{l}\cos iz=\cosh z,\ \sin iz=i\sinh z\\ \cosh iz=\cos z,\ \sinh iz=i\sin z\end{array}\right\} \qquad (4.22)$$

Finally, we examine the splitting of the elementary

[†] P. J. Hilton, *loc. cit.*, p. 30.

functions into real and imaginary parts. Let $z=x+iy$. Then

$$\exp z=\exp (x+iy)=e^x e^{iy}=e^x(\cos y+i \sin y),$$

so that

$$\mathscr{R}e^z=e^x\cos y, \quad \mathscr{I}e^z=e^x\sin y$$

$|e^z|=e^x$, $\arg e^z=y+2\pi k$, where k is that integer for which $-\pi<y+2\pi k\leqslant \pi$. Notice that the modulus of e^z depends only on the real part of z.

Next, by an application of (4.18) we find that

$$\sin (x+iy)=\sin x \cosh y+i \cos x \sinh y,$$

whence

$$\mathscr{R}\sin z=\sin x \cosh y, \quad \mathscr{I}\sin z=\cos x \sinh y,$$

$$|\sin z|^2=\sin^2 x \cosh^2 y+ \cos^2 x \sinh^2 y$$
$$=\sin^2 x (1+\sinh^2 y)+\cos^2 x \sinh^2 y$$
$$=\sin^2 x+(\sin^2 x+\cos^2 x) \sinh^2 y=\sin^2 x+\sinh^2 y,$$

so that

$$|\sin z|=(\sin^2 x+\sinh^2 y)^{\frac{1}{2}}.$$

The reader will have no difficulty in deriving the corresponding formulae for $\cos (x+iy)$ and for the other trigonometric functions.

6. THE LOGARITHM

All logarithms in this book refer to the base e. We recall that if x is positive, $\log x$ is that number u for which $x=\exp u$. It is known that there is one and only one real number with this property, so that $\log x$ is unambiguously defined as the real solution, for u, of the equation

$$x=\exp u,$$

where x is a given positive number.

By analogy, let us try to define $\log z$ as the solution, for w, of the equation

$$z=\exp w, \qquad (4.23)$$

where z is a given complex number. However, we now meet with the difficulty that, if w is a solution of (4.23), so is $w+2\pi ik$, where k is an arbitrary integer (see (2.21)). It follows that if $w=\log z$ exists at all, it has infinitely many values differing from one another by integral multiples of $2\pi i$. Let us now examine these values more closely.

Since exp w is never zero, no meaning can be attached to log z, when $z=0$. Accordingly we shall henceforth assume that $z \neq 0$. Write $z=r \exp (i\theta)$ and $w=u+iv$. Then (4.23) becomes

$$r\, e^{i\theta}=e^u\, e^{iv}. \tag{4.24}$$

Comparing moduli, we find that $r=\exp u$ and therefore

$$u=\log r,$$

where the logarithm has the usual unique real value which exists because $r>0$. Equation (4.24) now becomes exp $i\theta$ $=\exp iv$, from which we can only deduce that

$$v=\theta+2\pi k,$$

where k is an integer. Remembering that $r=|z|$ and $\theta=\arg z$, we can express the final result in the form

$$\log z=\log |z|+i(\arg z+2\pi k), \tag{4.25}$$

where log $|z|$ on the right-hand side denotes the real logarithm.

The value that corresponds to $k=0$, is called the *principal value* of the logarithm, and it is sometimes distinguished by a different notation, such as

$$\text{Log } z=\log |z|+i \arg z.$$

The principal value reduces to the usual meaning of log $x(=\text{Log } x)$, when x is positive, because in that case $\arg x=0$.

Examples.

(i) $\log (-2)=\text{Log}|-2|+i \arg (-2)=\text{Log } 2+\pi i$.

(ii) $\text{Log } i=\text{Log } |i|+\arg i=\text{Log } 1+i\pi/2=i\pi/2$.

(iii) Solve $4\cos z=3+i$. The equation is equivalent to $2 \exp (iz)+2 \exp (-iz)=3+i$. Hence

$$2 \exp (2iz)-(3+i) \exp (iz)+2=0.$$

Regarding this as a quadratic for exp (iz) we find, after some calculations, that

FUNCTIONS OF A COMPLEX VARIABLE

exp $(iz)=1+i$ or $\frac{1}{2}-\frac{1}{2}i$, and hence either

$$iz=\log(1+i)=\tfrac{1}{2}\mathrm{Log}\,2+i\left(\frac{\pi}{4}+2\pi n\right),$$

$$z=\frac{8n+1}{4}\pi-\frac{i}{2}\mathrm{Log}\,2\quad(n=0,\ \pm1,\ \pm2,\ \ldots)$$

or

$$iz=\log(\tfrac{1}{2}-\tfrac{1}{2}i)=-\tfrac{1}{2}\mathrm{Log}\,2+i\left(-\frac{\pi}{4}+2\pi m\right),$$

$$z=\frac{8m-1}{4}\pi+\frac{i}{2}\mathrm{Log}\,2\quad(m=0,\ \pm1,\ \pm2,\ \ldots).$$

(iv) The equation $\tan z=i$ has no solution, even when z is complex. For if $z=z_0$ were a solution, it would follow that $\sin z_0=i\cos z_0$, $\sin^2 z_0=-\cos^2 z_0$, $\sin^2 z_0+\cos^2 z_0=0$, in contradiction to (4.20).

EXERCISES ON CHAPTER FOUR

1. Examine $\lim z_n$, as $n\to\infty$, in the following cases and find its value when it exists.

(i) $z_n=\left(\dfrac{1+in}{1+n}\right)^3$ (ii) $z_n=i^n$ (iii) $z_n=\left(\dfrac{1}{2}+\dfrac{4}{5}i\right)^n$

(iv) $z_n=\left(\cos\dfrac{\pi}{n+1}+i\sin\dfrac{\pi}{n+1}\right)^n$ (v) $z_n=\tan in$.

2. Discuss the convergence of the following series.

(i) $\displaystyle\sum\frac{1}{n^2-in}$ (ii) $\displaystyle\sum\frac{n}{n^2+i}$ (iii) $\displaystyle\sum e^{in}\Big/n^2$

(iv) $\displaystyle\sum\left(\frac{2+3i}{4+i}\right)^n$ (v) $\displaystyle\sum\frac{\sin in}{n^2}$

3. Find the radius of convergence of the following power series.

(i) $\displaystyle\sum nz^n$ (ii) $\displaystyle\sum\frac{3^n-1}{2^n+1}z^n$ (iii) $\displaystyle\sum\frac{(2n)!z^n}{(n!)^2}$

(iv) $\displaystyle\sum\frac{\cos in}{n^2}z^n$

4. The power series $\Sigma a_n z^n$ and $\Sigma b_n z^n$ are such that $|b_n|\leqslant|a_n|(n=0, 1, 2, \ldots)$. Prove that the radius of convergence of the first power series cannot exceed that of the second.

5. Show that if z lies on the circle $x^2+y^2-2x-2y-2=0$, then $e^{-1}\leqslant|e^z|\leqslant e^3$.

6. Evaluate:
   (i) $\log(-1)$, (ii) $\log(1 - i \tan \alpha)(0 < \alpha < \tfrac{1}{2}\pi)$, (iii) 2^i, (iv) i^i.

7. Solve the equation $\sin z = 2$.

8. Prove that:
   (i) $2 \cosh z \cosh w = \cosh(z+w) + \cosh(z-w)$.
   (ii) $2 \sinh z \cosh w = \sinh(z+w) + \sinh(z-w)$.
   (iii) $2 \sinh z \sinh w = \cosh(z+w) - \cosh(z-w)$.

9. (i) Find the real and imaginary parts of $\tanh z$ $(= \sinh z / \cosh z$ where $z = x + iy$ $(x, y$ real$)$.
   (ii) Solve the equation $\tanh z = i$.

10. Show that if r is real and $|r| < 1$, then
$$\sin \theta + r \sin 3\theta + r^2 \sin 5\theta + \ldots = \frac{(1+r)\sin\theta}{1 - 2r\cos 2\theta + r^2}.$$
Deduce that if θ is not an integral multiple of $\tfrac{1}{2}\pi$
$$\sin\theta + \cos 2\theta \sin 3\theta + (\cos 2\theta)^2 \sin 5\theta + \ldots = \tfrac{1}{2}\operatorname{cosec}\theta.$$

Answers to Exercises

Chapter I

1. (i) $-5+10i$, (ii) $\dfrac{3}{13}-\dfrac{2}{13}i$, (iii) $-7+24i$, (iv) $\dfrac{7}{130}+\dfrac{2}{65}i$, (v) $\dfrac{11}{5}-\dfrac{2}{5}i$, (vi) $-i$.

2. (i) $1-i$, (ii) $3-2i$.

3. $n(n-1)+in^2$.

4. (i) 5, (ii) $|2-i|^6=(\sqrt{5})^6=125$, (ii) $|5+12i|^{-1}=\{\sqrt{(25+144)}\}^{-1}=1/13$, (iv) 1.

5. $\left|\dfrac{\alpha}{\beta}\right|=\left|\alpha\dfrac{1}{\beta}\right|=|\alpha|\left|\dfrac{1}{\beta}\right|=|\alpha|\dfrac{1}{|\beta|}$
$\dfrac{|1+2i|^{12}}{|1-2i|^9}=\dfrac{(\sqrt{5})^{12}}{(\sqrt{5})^9}=(\sqrt{5})^3=5\sqrt{5}$.

6. (i) $\pm\left(\dfrac{1}{\sqrt{2}}+\dfrac{i}{\sqrt{2}},\right)$ (ii) $\pm\{(\sqrt{2}+1)^{\frac{1}{2}}+i(\sqrt{2}-1)^{\frac{1}{2}}\}$, (iii) $\pm(2+i)$.

7. $2-i$, $1+2i$.

8. $\xi^2-4\xi+5=0$, roots $2+i$, $2-i$.

10. $\pm\frac{1}{2}(\sqrt{6}\pm\sqrt{2}i)$ (four combinations of signs).

Chapter II

1. If X is represented by x, the condition is that $(a-x)/(b-x)$ should be purely imaginary: $x=3$.

3. Interior and circumference of ellipse with foci at 1 and i and major axis 4.

4. The conditions are equivalent to $(z_1-z_3)/(z_3-z_2)=\lambda$ (see Example 2, p. 25).

6. By the well-known property of cyclic quadrilaterals it suffices to show that the sum of opposite angles, say at z_1 and z_3, is equal to π. Thus
$\arg(z_2-z_1)/(z_4-z_1)+\arg(z_4-z_3)/(z_2-z_3)=\pm\pi$ or 0
$\arg(z_2-z_1)(z_4-z_3)/(z_4-z_1)(z_2-z_3)=\pm\pi$ or 0,
that is $\{z_1, z_3; z_2, z_4\}$ is real.

7. $u-a=q(b-a)$, $v-b=u-a$.

8. When $\lambda=1$, that is when $|z-a|=|z-b|$, the equation represents all points equidistant from a and b, the perpendicular bisector of the segment AB.

10. $(-1)^m \left(\sec\dfrac{4m+1}{4n}\pi\right)^n (1+i)/\sqrt{2}$.

Chapter III

1. $1,\ \tfrac{1}{2}+\tfrac{1}{2}i\sqrt{3},\ -\tfrac{1}{2}+\tfrac{1}{2}i\sqrt{3},\ -1,\ -\tfrac{1}{2}-\tfrac{1}{2}i\sqrt{3},\ \tfrac{1}{2}-\tfrac{1}{2}i\sqrt{3}$.

2. $b,\ bi,\ -b,\ -bi$, where $b=\cos(\pi/8)+i\sin(\pi/8)$.

3. $\sqrt{2}\left(\cos\dfrac{\pi}{12}+i\sin\dfrac{\pi}{12}\right),\ -1+i,\ -\sqrt{2}\left(\cos\dfrac{5\pi}{12}+i\sin\dfrac{5\pi}{12}\right)$.

6. The sides of the triangle are represented by the vectors u, $v-u$, $-v$. Let $z=(-v)/u$, $w=(v-u)/u$. It is required to show that $\arg z=\pm 2\pi/3$, $\arg w=\pm 2\pi/3$. This follows from the fact that $z^2+z+1=w^2+w+1=0$.

7. Put $u=z_1-z_3$, $v=z_2-z_3$ (moving the origin to z_3).

8. In the product formula for z^8+1 divide each side by z^4 and put $z=e^{i\theta}$.

9. In the product formula for z^5+1 put $z=i$.

Chapter IV

1. (i) $-i$, (ii) no limit, (iii) 0, (iv) -1, (v) i.

2. (i) conv., (ii) div., because real parts div., (iii) abs. conv., (iv) conv., (v) div., because
$$\left|\frac{\sin in}{n^2}\right|=\left|\frac{e^{-n}-e^n}{2in^2}\right|>\frac{e^n-1}{2n^2}\to\infty.$$

3. (i) 1, (ii) $2/3$, (iii) $1/4$, (iv) $1/e$.

5. $|e^z|=e^x$. The greatest and least values of x on the circle are 3 and -1 respectively.

6. (i) $(2k+1)\pi i$ (ii) $\log\sec\alpha+i(-\alpha+2k\pi)$, (iii) $\cos\log 2+i\sin\log 2$ (iv) $\exp\left(-\tfrac{1}{2}\pi(4k+1)\right)$.

7. $(4k+1)\pi/2-i\log(2\pm\sqrt{3})$.

9. (i) $\dfrac{\sinh 2x+i\sin 2y}{\cosh 2x+\cos 2y}$, (ii) $\dfrac{4k+1}{4}\pi i$.

Index